The Glass Pantry

The Glass Pantry

THE PLEASURES OF SIMPLE PRESERVES

BY GEORGEANNE BRENNAN

PHOTOGRAPHY BY KATHRYN KLEINMAN

STYLING BY MICHAELE THUNEN

DESIGN BY JACQUELINE JONES DESIGN

CHRONICLE BOOKS

SAN FRANCISCO

Printed in Japan.

Library of Congress Cataloging-in-Publication Data

Brennan, Georgeanne, 1943-

    The glass pantry: the pleasures of simple preserves

    Georgeanne Brennan; photography by Kathryn Kleinman.

    p. cm.

    Includes bibliographical references and index.

    ISBN 0-8118-0388-0. – ISBN 0-8118-0393-7 (pbk.)

    1. Canning and preserving. I Title.

TX601.B734 1994

641.4'2–dc 20

93-15957

CIP

Editing by Sharon Silva

Design assistance and mechanical production by Kristen Jester
and Katie Nash, Jacqueline Jones Design

Distributed in Canada by

Raincoast Books

112 East Third Avenue

Vancouver, B.C.

V5T 1C8

10 9 8 7 6 5 4 3 2 1

Chronicle Books

275 Fifth Street

San Francisco, CA 94103

To my mother, Mary Brignell Kelly,
(1909 – 1993)
who gave me a love of literature,
food, and gardening
– Georgeanne

To Michael
and my children with love
– Kathryn

Table of Contents

79

Autumn

◆

Pomegranate Jelly

Pomegranate Vinegar

Pickled Crab Apples

Pears Pickled in Merlot

Figs Pickled in Balsamic Vinegar

and Herbes de Provence

Folie of Fall Fruits

Quince Slices in Vanilla Syrup

Zante Grapes in Armagnac

Salsa all'Agresto

Italian Wine Conserve

Pickled Mushrooms

Confit of Roasted Leeks

Goat Cheese in Olive Oil

and Herbs

Cracked Green Olives with Fennel

and Bay Leaves

Provençal Hot Chili Oil

◆

109

Winter

◆

Navel Orange Marmalade

Rose Hip Jelly

Candied Grapefruit Peel

Lemon Curd

Confit of Roasted Onions

Ancho Chili Sauce

Pickled Garlic Cloves

Pickled Whole Onions

Pink Pickled Shallots

Pickled Carrots

and Jalapeño Chilies

Whole Preserved Lemons

Spicy Lemon Oil

Vin d'Orange

Cayenne Walnuts

Salted Blanched Almonds

◆

Introduction

The preservation of special fruits and vegetables in small, manageable quanti-
ties solely for the pleasure of the process, of the taste, and for giving as gifts is far removed from the
necessity of preserving food. In the past, foods were salted or sugared, dried or packed in vinegar
brines or alcohol, or turned into sweet gels, then stored in cool, dark places to be drawn upon during
the cold months when fresh food was scarce. Many of these venerable methods were either forgotten or deemed old-fashioned, as modern home canning came to dominate food preservation in
the early years of the twentieth century, later to be replaced by home freezing.   ✦   Even though
it has been many decades since home preserving has been necessary, its primary image remains
the canning or freezing of large quantities of fruits and vegetables. Unfortunately, it is a portrait that
seems both irrelevant and unappealing, although the idea of reconnecting with the past, of taking
control of our kitchens and tables, does have appeal. *The Glass Pantry* is a response to this idea, to
the rediscovery of preserving that emphasizes the joys of simple, flavorful preparations.   ✦   Many

old-fashioned preserving methods are well matched to today's life-style. Capturing the taste of spring-time's tarragon or summer's basil in a flavored vinegar takes only long enough to put a handful of the herbs into a glass jar, but throughout the year the homemade vinegar can be used in salads or sauces as a reminder of those seasons. On a warm summer evening, pouring a small glass of winter's vin d'orange or sipping the syrup of spring's brandied cherries is an elegant testimony to one's own creativity and imagination, yet the initial preparation requires little more than putting the fruit into wine or brandy months earlier. ✦ To dry tomatoes, one needs to do no more than thinly slice them and set them in the sun. Months later, as one reaches for the glass jar where the tomatoes have been stored, the memories of summer come flooding back, to be savored again in deeply rich sauces that nap pastas and cover pizzas. Dried apricots are created just as easily and are intensely sweet and splendid enough to give as candy. ✦ Part of the glass pantry resides in the refrigerator. Relishes, chutneys, and confits of all kinds are stored there, ready to be taken out and spread onto sandwiches or spooned into sauces. Another part of the glass pantry is the traditional pantry storage shelf, today most likely a spot in a cool basement or garage. There stand paraffin-sealed glass jars, glistening with a distinctive jelly, perhaps rose geranium or pomegranate, alongside jars of thick cherry preserves and a jar or two of tiny Zante grapes resting in amber Armagnac. Here, too, are the canned preserves of sunny yellow tomato ketchup and Italian pickled beets, of apricots in Marsala, Italian roasted peppers, and herb-laced figs. ✦ Winter's sugared nuts and spring's candied rose petals need no special storage conditions. They are kept in the part of the glass pantry on display on the kitchen counter or living room table where they can be admired—and eaten—by everyone. ✦ I have strong memories of a certain cut-glass dish with a round, fitted lid and a prism knob that my grandmother used for the candied walnuts and grapefruit peels she made at Christmas time. We lived in southern California, in what was then a small beach town, and my grandmother lived inland, fifty miles distant. When she came to visit us, she always brought shopping bags heavy with mason jars filled with peaches, pears, plums, apricots, and green beans, each bearing stickers carefully labeled in script with the date of canning—month and year—and contents. My mother dutifully thanked her and put the jars away deep in the back of a kitchen cupboard, where most of them stayed until they were disposed of eventually. The excuse was always that they were probably too old to eat. ◆ Although there was no reason for my grandmother to can—she shopped twice a week at a large supermarket and went to a neighborhood grocery almost daily—it was a part of her life. As a child I hated to be served "grandma's canned peaches" because they didn't taste the same as the ones from the store, but I loved to climb the trees in her backyard and pick her peaches and other fruits. I would fill my pinafore skirt with the choicest ones, then clamber down the ladder to give them to her to inspect. Upon her approval, the fruits went into her gray metal bucket. I would then go back up the ladder and repeat the process until the bucket was full. ◆ Standing over her stove, in a sweltering-hot July kitchen, my grandmother, surrounded by buckets of fruit and dozens and dozens of empty glass jars, stirred cauldrons of chopped fruit for jam and simmered huge kettles of fruit to can whole. She tried to lure me into helping her, but I usually managed to beg off. It was just too hot in the kitchen. ◆ After my grandmother's death, the only canning I witnessed was my mother's yearly half-dozen jars of clove-pierced pickled peaches, which I liked, and a few jars of watermelon rind preserves, which I did not.　　✦　　It wasn't until I moved to the French countryside that I became interested in preserving food. The village in which I lived twenty years ago was remote, located at a crossroads in the back country of Provence. Few people had refrigerators, and none had freezers. Almost everyone had a *cave*, though, where a vaulted ceiling and two-foot-thick stone walls ensured a cool, even temperature throughout most of the year. Wine, olives, root vegetables, cured meat, and preserved foods of all kinds were kept in the *cave*. The venerable tradition of making one's own ham, pâté, and sausages was still strong, and everyone had a *potager*, or "kitchen garden," plus a few fruit trees. I was part of a rural life that had changed very little during half a century, in spite of two world wars fought across this land.　　✦　　Almost every inhabitant of the region was still close to the earth. The young married women my age, like their own mothers, dried fruits and vegetables, prepared their own olives, made jams and jellies from the wild berries gathered in the mountains, and put Montmorency cherries into brandy. These women didn't attempt to put up huge quantities of food, but rather strove to preserve in a special way the very best of each season. The treasures were brought out for guests and on celebratory occasions like Easter or a saint's day. I was enthralled by the whole direction and the pace of the life, and particularly fascinated by how simply and naturally food was treated and how good it tasted. ✦ Although I only lived in the village a few years, the experience was indelibly etched in my mind and it changed the way I thought about food. On returning home to California, I planted a potager and fruit and nut trees whenever I could, and sought out farmers' markets reminiscent of those in France. I have rarely repeated my grandmother's custom of canning huge quantities of food in mason jars, but the style of preserving I learned first in the French countryside is part of my life.

About Preserving

Food is preserved to extend its life by slowly or temporarily stopping the process of decay. For thousands of years, man has preserved food by the simple methods of salting, drying, pickling, and saturation with sugar or alcohol. In these five basic techniques, the moisture content is altered and environments inhospitable to the agents responsible for decay, enzyme activity, and microbes are created. Generally, these preserved foods need to be stored in cool, dry locations, as moisture and warmth spur decay.

In modern home canning, food is preserved by being brought to high temperatures in sealed glass containers and kept at those temperatures long enough to kill any microbes and to stop destructive enzyme activity. The containers become hermetically sealed during the process, which prevents reinfection and allows properly canned food to be stored at room temperature with no risk of spoilage.

The types of preserves included in this book are described in the following pages, along with any special equipment needed to make them and some general storage information. This is not meant to be a complete guide to home preserving. For example, freezing, a common method of preserving food, is not discussed at all. This is instead a reference to be used in conjunction with the recipes for the special, seasonal preserves and other foods in The Glass Pantry.

A Guide to the Glass Pantry

There are a number of different types of culinary treasures stored in the glass pantry. They are identified here. The differences between them are sometimes only fine ones.

JAMS, PRESERVES, MARMALADES, AND JELLIES

These preparations are all variations on a gel, usually made with a combination of fruit and fruit juices boiled with sugar. While sugar is the preserving element in each case, pectin in combination with sugar and acid is responsible for jelling. Fruits contain natural pectin in varying degrees. Some fruits, such as citrus, sour plums, tart apples, quinces, and grapes, contain sufficient pectin to jell. Other low-pectin fruits generally need the addition of pectin to accomplish jelling.

Commercial pectin is available in powdered or liquid form. It needs to be used in combination with large amounts of sugar, making the resulting gels too sweet for many tastes. With the exception of the recipe for tart pomegranate jelly, I have opted for achieving jelling by adding high-pectin fruits, such as quinces or tart apples, to low-pectin fruits, or by specifying the use of slightly underripe fruits, which are higher in pectin than fully ripe ones. To boost acidity in low-acid fruits, I have added lemon juice.

Jam, made by boiling pieces of fruit or whole soft fruits together with sugar, fruit juice, and water, is quite easy to prepare. The fruit dissolves and combines with the gel to make it opaque. Preserves are made in the same way, but whole fruits or large, distinct pieces of fruit are used and they remain intact, while the gel itself remains transparent or semitransparent. (The word *preserves* is also used as a general term for jams, jellies, and other fruit spreads.)

Marmalade is generally prepared by boiling the pulp of citrus fruits with sugar and very fine bits of the peel, which remain suspended in the semitransparent gel. Jelly, which is transparent, or nearly so, is made by boiling concentrated juice with sugar.

No special equipment is needed to make jam, marmalade, or preserves. To make jelly, you will need a jelly bag or several layers of cheesecloth for straining the juice.

CONSERVES

A conserve is essentially a jam made of two or more kinds of fruits to which nuts and possibly dried fruits, such as raisins, have been added. Although conserves can usually be stored in the refrigerator for several weeks, for long-term storage they should be processed in a hot-water bath.

CHUTNEYS

Chutneys are pickled mixtures of pieces of fruit (often several different kinds) cooked with sugar, vinegar, spices, and herbs until thickened. Like conserves, chutneys can be stored in the refrigerator for a good length of time, but for long-term storage they should be processed in a hot-water bath.

BRANDIED FRUITS

Whole fruits or pieces of fruit can be preserved in alcohol, an environment in which microbes cannot live. The fruit is simply immersed in distilled spirits of 80 proof (40 percent alcohol), such as brandy, Cognac, eau-de-vie, gin, or vodka. Often a little sugar is added, as well. This is done either by putting sugar into the jar along with the fruit and allowing it to dissolve, or by first making a syrup with the sugar and a little of the alcohol. The covered jars are stored in a cool, dark place.

Brandied fruits will keep for a year or longer. No special equipment is required for making them.

FRUITS IN SYRUP

Whole or sliced fruits—generally firm fruits that will retain their shape—are cooked in a light, medium, or heavy syrup. Juice, wine, herbs, or spices are sometimes added, as well. The cooked fruit will keep refrigerated for several days, but for long-term storage the fruit must be processed in a hot-water bath.

INFUSED WINES

Simple flavored wines are made by adding fruits, herbs, or spices to red, white, or rosé wines. Sugar and distilled spirits are added as well, and the wine is put in a cool, dark place for twenty-four hours to thirty days. It is then strained and rebottled.

Infused wines will keep for up to one year when stored in a cool, dark place. No special equipment is needed for making infused wines other than wine bottles and corks.

INFUSED VINEGARS

Vinegar is flavored in much the same way wine is. Fruits, herbs, or spices are added to vinegar of any kind. The vinegar is then put in a sunny spot or other warm location until it becomes sufficiently flavored, generally about ten days. The vinegar is strained, rebottled, and stored in a cool, dark place.

Infused vinegars will keep for six months or longer. No special equipment is needed for making flavored vinegars.

INFUSED OILS

As with flavored wines and vinegars, fruits, herbs, or spices are put into oil and left there until the oil has become sufficiently infused with their flavor. The oil is then strained, rebottled, and stored in a cool, dark place.

These infused oils will keep for six months or longer. No special equipment is needed for making them.

VEGETABLE CONFITS

Thin slices or pieces of vegetables are cooked slowly in fat, commonly olive oil or butter, but occasionally lard or other animal fats, along with a little sugar, salt, and sometimes herbs, until the vegetables virtually dissolve and caramelize somewhat. Confits will keep in tightly capped containers in a refrigerator for a week or more.

PICKLES

Pickles are fruits or vegetables, either whole or in pieces, that have absorbed enough acid, most commonly the acetic acid in vinegar, to slow down microbial activity. To do this, however, the vinegar must be of at least 4 percent strength. Do not use homemade vinegar, as its strength cannot be accurately determined. Salt, spices, herbs, and sometimes sugar are added to the vinegar. Brines composed of salt and water are used to make fermented pickles, which are outside the scope of this book. Ketchups belong to the pickle category, as do relishes. In general, no special equipment is needed for pickle making.

Although pickles will keep refrigerated or in other cold-storage conditions for a short time, for long-term storage, pickles must be processed in a hot-water bath.

SEALING TECHNIQUES AND EQUIPMENT

In the home canning of fruits and vegetables, cooked or uncooked fruits or vegetables are packed into glass jars and capped with lids that will eventually form a hermetic seal (see page 23 for information on types of jars). The jars are heated in a hot-water bath until their interior temperatures are high enough to kill microbes and to stop enzyme activity. The jars hermetically seal during the process and the atmosphere in the jars becomes anaerobic. Harmful microbes capable of living in high-acid foods—most fruits, tomatoes, and pickled fruit or vegetable preparations—are destroyed after being processed in boiling water, that is, in water that reaches 212 degrees F. The length of time foods are processed depends upon the acidity of the food and the size of the jar or jars. Large jars take longer than small jars. The tight seal prevents contamination from new organisms, and the canned, high-acid foods may be safely stored at room temperature.

Clostridium botulinum produces the deadly toxin that causes botulism. The bacteria thrive in an anaerobic environment, but cannot live in a high-acid environment, which makes canned, high-acid foods safe from the risk of botulism.

Low-acid foods, however, are hospitable to harmful microbes, including Clostridium botulinum, that are not destroyed in a hot-water bath of 212 degrees F. Low-acid foods include meats and most vegetables, with the exception of tomatoes. To achieve the high temperatures necessary to destroy low-acid bacteria requires special pressure canning equipment. None of the recipes in this book are for low-acid foods or food preparations.

COLD-PACK AND HOT-PACK FOODS

There are basically two methods for packing foods into jars for processing. If the food in the jar is hot and then covered with a hot liquid, it is a hot pack. It is also a hot pack if the food is cold or raw, yet is covered with hot liquid. Hot-pack jars go directly into the boiling water of a hot-water bath and the timing is started immediately. If the food is cold—cooked or raw—and covered with a cold liquid, it is a cold pack. Cold-pack jars are put into cold water and the processing time starts from the moment the water reaches a boil.

THE HOT-WATER BATH

For hot-pack foods, have the water boiling in a canning kettle or other large pot. Ladle the prepared food into clean, dry glass jars with lids that will form hermetic seals. Using long-handled tongs or a jar holder, lower the filled jars into the boiling water. Make sure the jars are not touching either the bottom of the kettle or pot or one another. Add additional boiling water if necessary to ensure that the tops of the jars are covered by at least a half inch of boiling water. Cover the pot and process the number of minutes directed in the specific recipe. Add more boiling water, if necessary, to keep the jars submerged.

If processing cold-pack foods, lower the filled jars into enough cold water to cover them by at least a half inch. Cover, bring to a boil, and process the number of minutes directed in the specific recipe.

When the processing period has ended, remove the jars and let them cool for twelve hours or overnight, then check for a complete seal. As screw-top ring lids seal, there is often an audible "ping." Also, the lid will be slightly concave if the seal is complete. On a glass-lidded jar, the seal has taken if you cannot readily lift up the glass lid.

Although foods processed in a water bath may be stored at room temperature, storing them in a cool, dark place protects the foods from discoloration.

THE JELLY METHOD

The *jell point* is the term used to describe when preserves, particularly jellies, have reached the temperature at which they are properly thickened and are ready to be put into jars. I strongly recommend using a candy thermometer for this test; it will read 220 degrees F when the jell point has been reached. The thermometer is easy and foolproof, but if you lack one, a simple visual test can be used: Scoop up a spoonful of the simmering mixture and, holding the spoon horizontally, slowly rotate it. Allow the liquid to fall off the spoon back into the pot, watching the drops along the lower edge of the spoon. When the mixture has jelled properly, it will coat the spoon and fall from its side in a single sheet without dripping. At this point, the mixture can be ladled into hot, dry, sterilized jars and sealed.

SEALING WITH PARAFFIN

A thin disk of melted paraffin wax makes an effective barrier against the moisture and evaporation that causes surface molds to form on jellies and other thick preserves. To prepare these disks, melt chunks of paraffin in a heatproof container reserved only for this purpose. A small saucepan or coffee pot, without a lid, is ideal, because the hot paraffin is easily poured from either vessel.

Since paraffin is highly flammable, do not put the container over direct heat. Instead, place the container in a pan of simmering water, stirring the paraffin as it melts.

To form the paraffin layer, first carefully wipe the rim of the jar clean. Then pour a layer of hot paraffin, one-eighth-inch thick, onto the surface of the preserve, covering it completely to form a thin disk that seals the jar. Prick any air bubbles with a needle. Allow the first layer to harden, then pour on a second layer of equal thickness.

Let the jars stand overnight to allow the paraffin to harden fully before adding other coverings such as waxed paper or cloth and before storing. As the paraffin hardens, it forms a seal along the edges of the jar, becomes opaque, and develops a slight depression in the middle of the disk. In the case of an incomplete seal, remove the failed disk and repeat the process.

Store any unused paraffin in the container and remelt when needed. If you prefer not to use paraffin, sealable lids can be used in its place and the jars can be processed in a hot-water bath.

EQUIPMENT

The recipes in this book can be accomplished with little or no special equipment. Specially designed water-bath canners with lids and wire racks for holding six jars are available. They come in different sizes for handling different-size jars, ranging from half-pint to two quart. Although I have one of these kettles, I find I more often use a stockpot fitted with a cake rack because it is better suited to processing a single large jar or two or three small ones. Also, I have yet to find a kettle that can accommodate the large, beautifully styled European-made canning jars that I like so much and that are now readily available in the United States.

If you are using a conventional pot, select a lidded one deep enough to hold the canning jars with room for them to be covered by at least a half-inch of boiling water. Place a rack in the pot so the jars will not be resting on the pot bottom and wrap kitchen towels around the jars to prevent them from touching during the water bath.

I recommend having on hand a good pair or two of tongs for gripping jars that must be lowered into or be lifted out of the water bath. A candy thermometer is handy for checking the jell point. I love using the thermometer because I trust it completely to indicate when the proper temperature is reached. For jelly making (but not for other gels such as jams and marmalades), a jelly bag or several layers of cheesecloth are necessary to obtain the clear, concentrated juice needed.

For making both sweetened fruit preserves and vegetable preparations, I generally use heavy-bottomed stainless-steel saucepans or soup pots, depending upon the quantity of preserves I am making. Any standard kitchen pots and pans will do, however, except those made from reactive materials, such as nonenameled cast iron or nonanodized aluminum. Although a classic copper preserving kettle would be beautiful as well as useful to have, especially if one were cooking large quantities, it is not necessary.

Two kinds of glass canning jars can be used. The type most commonly seen in the United States has a two-piece metal top consisting of a screw-top ring and a flat lid with an inner rubber lip. The other jar, customarily used in Europe and increasingly available here, has a glass lid attached with wire and bales. A rubber ring is placed around the mouth of the jar to create the seal. Each time a jar is used for canning purposes, a new rubber-lipped lid or rubber ring, depending upon the type of jar, must be used to ensure a complete seal.

Jellies and other thick preserves that will be sealed with paraffin can be put into a wide variety of jars and glasses. These containers must, however, be able to withstand the heat of sterilization.

STERILIZING THE EQUIPMENT

An ideal and simple way to sterilize bottles, canning jars, and lids is to put them through the cycle on an automatic dishwasher. Alternatively, wash everything in hot, sudsy water, rinse well, and then boil in clear water to cover for five minutes.

Drain jars well before filling and ensure that they are dry, as moisture may cause mold to form. Jars that will be sealed with paraffin should be both dry and still hot when they are filled. If a paraffin seal fails, however, the disk may be removed and the sealing repeated even though the jar and its contents have cooled.

Although it never hurts to sterilize any jars before filling them with preserves, I generally do not sterilize jars that are destined for a hot-water bath. I believe clean, dry jars work fine because sterilization takes place during the high temperatures reached in the water bath.

A COOL, DARK PLACE

This term occurs in many of the storage instructions in this and other books about preserves. A cool place is one where the temperature remains between 32 degrees and 45 degrees F. A dark place is one that is shielded from direct sunlight or any other constant light source.

SPRING

✦

✦

In the Spring . . .

By the time a new spring arrives, the wares of the previous spring are gone from the pantry. On a sunny winter morning, the last of the cherry preserves were served to friends who stopped by unexpectedly on their way to the mountains. The brandied cherries were ladled into beautiful jars and given as Christmas gifts, as were the frosted bottles of tarragon vinegar. The spring apricots, dried in the even sun of May and early June, went to fill Thanksgiving turkeys and holiday cookies. Well before fall turned cold, the pickled artichokes had been eaten.   ✦   The new spring brings, of course, a wealth of artichokes, cherries, and apricots, along with new flushes of herbs and a burgeoning crop of wild greens to gather from the roadside. It is only after feasting substantially upon these in their fresh state that my thoughts can turn to preserving my seasonal favorites. Soon the glass jars and bottles are brought up from the basement to be sorted and washed and lined up in a row on my kitchen counter. Throughout spring I periodically bring in a basketful of artichokes and delicate red-and-white radishes from the garden, or carefully picked fruits from neighboring orchards, for packing into those sparkling clean containers.   ✦   Living as I do in the remnants of one of California's great fruit-producing regions, I have access to plantings of the indescribably sweet Royal Blenheim and Royal Derby apricots, the standard of taste in the early days of this century before the development of early shipping varieties rendered them obsolete. ✦ Cherries, spring's other special fruit, come in shades of dark purple, red, yellow, and yellow blushed with red to pink. All of them are good for making preserves, jams, fortified wines, and jellies. For brandying, though, I prefer the small, sour morellos or the French Montmorency cherries. Their color, tart taste, and firm flesh are reminiscent of the wild cherries that grow in the mountains of Provence, which I so happily gathered and packed into eau-de-vie when I lived there. ✦ Well before summer's heat has begun to build, the jars and bottles, now full, are carried back down the cellar steps to be placed in the cool dark, alongside winter's cavalcade of vin d'orange and pickled shallots and onions.

Green Almond Conserve

YEARS AGO AN ITALIAN FARMER OFFERED ME MY FIRST GREEN ALMOND, SHOWING ME HOW TO CRACK OPEN THE FURRY, YOUNG HULL AND FIBROUS SHELL WITH MY TEETH AND EXTRACT THE BARELY FORMED NUT INSIDE. THE SMOOTH, IVORY KERNEL WAS TENDER AND TASTED LIKE PURE ALMOND, WITHOUT THE DRY AND GRAINY TEXTURE OF THE MATURE NUT.

FOR TRUE AFICIONADOS OF GREEN ALMONDS, THE PRIME MOMENT IS WHEN THE SEED CASE HAS JUST BEGUN TO PLUMP, THE INTERIOR IS STILL LIQUID, AND THERE IS NO HINT OF A SHELL. THE WHOLE ALMOND, INCLUDING THE GREEN HULL, IS SERVED CHILLED, SOMETIMES IN SALTED ICE WATER, AND EATEN WITH A LITTLE SALT.

IN THIS RECIPE THE GREEN ALMONDS ARE CHOPPED AND COMBINED IN A SPICED MIXTURE WITH DATES AND RAISINS TO MAKE A CONSERVE. THE INTENSE ALMOND TASTE CONTRASTS WELL WITH THE DENSE, RICH BACKGROUND OF THE OTHER INGREDIENTS. THE CONSERVE CAN BE SPREAD ON BUTTERED BREAD FOR TEATIME OR SPOONED ALONGSIDE GRILLED EGGPLANT AND PEPPERS FOR A SWEET-AND-SAVORY COMBINATION. IT ALSO MAKES A GOOD FILLING FOR COOKIES.

◆

50 to 60 green almonds at the soft
nut stage (about 1¹/₂ pounds),
or ¹/₂ cup unsalted
mature shelled almonds
1 cup raisins
1 cup distilled white vinegar
1 cup loosely packed brown sugar
8 to 10 large Medjool dates
(about ¹/₂ pound),
pitted and coarsely chopped
1 cup water
6 whole cloves, crushed

◆

Using a sharp knife, slice through the green almonds lengthwise, splitting the interior nut in half. Pick out the ivory nut halves with the knife tip and set aside. Do not be concerned if some of the nuts are still in the semiliquid stage. Set aside 8 halves and coarsely chop the remainder. If you are using mature almonds, chop all of them.

Combine the raisins and the vinegar in a nonreactive saucepan and let stand for 10 minutes. Place over medium-low heat, bring to a simmer, and cook for 5 to 6 minutes. Add the sugar, dates, water, and cloves and cook for another 5 minutes. Then add the green or mature almonds and simmer for 2 to 3 minutes. The mixture will be rather thick and dense.

Remove from the heat and spoon into a hot, dry, sterilized jar with a lid. Tuck the reserved green almond halves along the walls of the jar, making a decorative band or arrangement. Cover with the lid.

Store in the refrigerator. The conserve will keep for up to 2 weeks.

Makes 1 pint

Whole Apricots in Marsala

$\mathcal{P}$ACKED INTO JARS AND COVERED WITH A SWEET MARSALA SYRUP, UNPITTED

PLUMP APRICOTS TAKE ON A RICH, DEEP GOLD AS THEY ABSORB THE SYRUP. USE SLIGHTLY

UNDERRIPE APRICOTS, AS THEY BETTER RETAIN THEIR SHAPE AND TEXTURE DURING COOKING.

SERVED ON THEIR OWN, ACCOMPANIED WITH A CRUNCHY COOKIE OR TWO, OR SPOONED

OVER ICE CREAM, THESE MARSALA-INFUSED APRICOTS ARE A SIMPLE DESSERT, ALREADY

PREPARED AND WAITING IN THE PANTRY. THEY ARE ALSO AN APPROPRIATE ACCOMPANIMENT

TO RICH MEATS, SUCH AS ROAST PORK.

◆

2 pounds firm,

slightly underripe apricots

³/₄ cup water

1¹/₂ cups granulated sugar

Juice of 1 lemon

2 tablespoons grated lemon zest

2 whole cloves

1¹/₄ cups Marsala

¹/₈ teaspoon ground cinnamon

◆

Using a sharp needle, prick the surface of each apricot in several places. Set aside.

Combine the water and sugar in a stainless-steel or other nonreactive saucepan over medium heat. Bring to a boil, stirring constantly until the sugar melts; this should take 3 to 4 minutes. Reduce the heat and simmer until a thin syrup forms, about 10 minutes. Add the lemon juice and zest, cloves, and Marsala. Simmer for 4 or 5 minutes. Remove from the heat and let cool to room temperature.

Using a slotted spoon, remove the whole apricots and pack them as tightly as possible into clean, dry jars with sealable lids. Stir the cinnamon into the cooled syrup, then pour the syrup over the apricots, filling the jars to within ½ inch of the rims. Using a damp cloth, wipe the rims clean. Cover with the lids and process for 30 minutes in a hot-water bath (see instructions for processing cold-pack foods on page 21).

Remove the jars and let them cool for 12 hours or overnight. Check the lids for a complete seal.

Store the sealed jars in a cool, dark place. The apricots will keep for up to 1 year. Once opened, keep them refrigerated. Store any jar lacking a good seal in the refrigerator for up to 10 days.

Makes about 3 pints

Whole Cherry Preserves

CHERRIES ARE NATURALLY LOW IN PECTIN. IN ORDER FOR THEM TO JELL WHEN COOKED WITH ONLY SUGAR OR HONEY, THEY MUST BE SIMMERED LONG AND SLOWLY OVER VERY LOW HEAT, IN THE MANNER THAT CHERRY PRESERVES ARE STILL TRADITIONALLY MADE IN THE FRENCH AND GERMAN COUNTRYSIDES. DURING COOKING, THE CHERRIES BECOME PROFOUNDLY SWEET AND CHEWY, AND EVERY SPOONFUL TASTES LIKE FRUIT AND SUN REDUCED TO A SINGLE FLAVOR.

◆

2 pounds ripe sweet cherries
such as Bing or Lambert
3½ cups granulated sugar
2 cups water
1 star anise
2 tablespoons honey

◆

Discard any blemished cherries. Remove and discard the stems from the cherries. Pit them by gently squeezing each fruit until the pit pops out, leaving the cherry whole. If the pit does not pop out easily, slit the cherry open with a knife and pick out the pit. A cherry pitter may also be used, but it mangles the cherries more than the hand method does, and I find that it takes me only about 15 minutes to pit 2 pounds of cherries using the hand method. Set the pitted cherries aside.

Put the sugar and water in a large, heavy-bottomed stainless-steel or other nonreactive pot. Let stand, stirring occasionally, until the sugar dissolves, 5 or 10 minutes. Add the star anise and simmer over low heat, stirring from time to time, for 15 minutes. Remove the star anise and stir in the pitted cherries and the honey. Raise the heat and bring to a boil. Then again reduce the heat to low and simmer for about 1¾ hours, increasing the heat to medium-low after about 1½ hours. Be careful the preserves do not scorch.

After the first 45 minutes of cooking, begin to test for the jell point (see instructions on page 22). Alternatively, insert a candy thermometer in the mixture. When it reads 220 degrees F, the preserves are ready.

Remove from the heat. Skim off and discard any surface foam. Ladle the preserves into hot, dry, sterilized jars, filling to within ½ inch of the rims. Seal with a ⅛-inch-thick layer of melted paraffin (see directions for working with paraffin on page 22). Allow that layer to harden, then add a second layer of the same thickness. Using a damp cloth, wipe the rims clean. Cover with lids, aluminum foil, or with waxed paper or cotton cloth tightly fastened with twine or a rubber band.

Store in a cool, dark place. The preserves will keep for up to 1 year.

Makes about 4 pints

Wild Greens and Garlic Relish

No MATTER WHERE YOU LIVE,
SPRING WILL BRING A PROFUSION OF WILD
GREENS. FOR CENTURIES, THE FIRST GREENS
WERE THE SIGNAL THAT THE THRALL OF WINTER
HAD ENDED AND THAT SPRING, SUMMER, AND
FALL WOULD HOLD COURT ONCE MORE. THE
KNOWLEDGE OF WHICH GREENS WERE EDIBLE AND
WHICH WERE NOT HAS BEEN PASSED FROM
GENERATION TO GENERATION, AND EVEN TODAY
IN EUROPE ONE CAN SEE PEOPLE OF ALL AGES
OUT WITH GATHERING BASKETS, SEARCHING
ALONG ROADSIDES AND THE EDGES OF CULTI-
VATED FIELDS FOR SUCH DELICACIES AS YOUNG
PURSLANE, CHICORY, DANDELION, MUSTARD,
AND CRESS.

HERE, THE GREENS ARE MADE INTO A
RELISH—MORE A PURÉE THAN A TYPICAL
CHOPPED RELISH—THAT IS A GOOD ACCOMPANI-
MENT TO POACHED TROUT OR SALMON. I LIKE TO
STIR A TEASPOONFUL INTO A VINAIGRETTE
DRESSING, TOO.

12 cups firmly packed mixed
greens such as dandelion,
arugula, purslane, watercress,
and sorrel, leaves only
2 cloves garlic, minced
2 teaspoons salt
1¹⁄₂ cups white wine vinegar

Mince the greens and
combine them in a glass
bowl with the garlic, 1
teaspoon of the salt, and
1 cup of the vinegar.
Cover the bowl and
refrigerate overnight.

The next day, squeeze
the greens dry and pack
them tightly into a small,
dry, sterilized jar with a
lid. Combine the remain-
ing 1 teaspoon salt and
½ cup vinegar in a
nonreactive saucepan.
Bring to a boil over high
heat and boil for 3 to 4
minutes to make a brine.
Remove from the heat
and let the brine cool
completely.

Pour the cooled brine
over the greens. Cover
with the lid and store in
the refrigerator. The
relish will keep for up to
4 weeks.

Makes about 1½ cups

Pickled Artichokes

I HAVEN'T THE SLIGHTEST SHRED OF HESITATION IN SAYING THAT THESE PICKLES ARE WORTH EVERY BIT OF EFFORT NEEDED TO MAKE THEM. WITHOUT QUESTION, THEY ARE ONE OF THE BEST-TASTING AND MOST BEAUTIFUL GLASS JARS ON THE PANTRY SHELF. THE PALE, CREAMY YELLOW LEAVES THAT SURROUND EACH ARTICHOKE HEART GLISTEN IN THE OIL-AND-HERB-VINEGAR PICKLING SOLUTION. SOMETIMES THE FAINT HINT OF PURPLE ON THE CHOKE, THE EVENTUAL FLOWER BUD, IS EVIDENT, TOO.

SINCE I USE THE ARTICHOKES FROM MY GARDEN, I CAN PICK THE TINIEST BUDS, NO LARGER THAN A BIG MARBLE, AND PICKLE THEM WHOLE. PACKED IN JARS, THESE WHOLE BUDS MAKE SPOTS OF DARK GREEN AMONG THE YELLOW. SEASONED WITH OREGANO, BASIL, BAY LEAVES, GARLIC, AND SOMETIMES DRIED RED CHILIES, THE PICKLED ARTICHOKES HAVE A RUSTIC TASTE THAT RECALLS THE SIMPLE ANTIPASTI OF ITALY'S COUNTRY TRATTORIAS.

2 cups fresh lemon juice

4 cups water

36 to 40 small artichokes

3 lemons, halved

4 cups distilled white vinegar

$1/2$ teaspoon salt

2 cloves garlic

4 fresh or dried bay leaves

$1/2$ teaspoon dried basil

$1/2$ teaspoon dried oregano

2 to 4 small dried red chili peppers

(optional)

2 cups olive oil

Combine the lemon juice and water in a non-reactive saucepan large enough to hold the trimmed artichokes eventually. Prepare the artichokes one at a time: Trim the stem end, leaving   to 1 inch of the stem intact. Halve the artichoke from tip to stem end. Immediately rub the cut surface with a lemon half to prevent discoloring. Scoop out the furry choke, then gently rub the newly exposed surface with lemon. Cut off the outer layers of leaves, so the only leaves remaining are the tender, pale yellow ones. Older or larger artichokes have more tough outer leaves and a more fully developed choke and may need to be trimmed down until only the tender heart remains. Immediately drop the trimmed artichoke into the saucepan filled with lemon water. Repeat this process until all the artichokes have been trimmed. It is no wonder that this is often a family endeavor in the Mediterranean countries—and at my house, too!

Bring the lemon water and artichokes to a simmer over medium heat. Cook for 3 to 5 minutes, depending upon the size of the artichoke pieces. If mixed sizes are used, remove the small ones after 3 minutes.

Drain the artichoke pieces and pack them tightly into 2 clean, dry pint jars with sealable lids. Add 1 cup of the vinegar and   teaspoon of the salt to each jar. Cover with the lids and let stand overnight.

The next day, drain off the vinegar and discard. Pour 1 cup fresh vinegar into each jar and cover with the lids. Let the jars stand at room temperature for 4 to 8 hours.

Drain off the vinegar again and add 1 garlic clove, 2 bay leaves, and   teaspoon each of the basil and oregano and 1 or 2 chili peppers (if using) to each jar. Pour in olive oil to within   inch of the rims. Using a damp cloth, wipe the rims clean. Cover with the lids and process for 30 minutes in a hot-water bath (see instructions for processing cold-pack foods on page 21).

Remove the jars and let them cool for 12 hours or overnight. Check the lids for a complete seal.

Store the sealed jars in a cool, dark place. The artichokes will keep for up to 1 year. Once opened, keep them refrigerated, but bring to room temperature before using. Store any jar lacking a good seal in the refrigerator for up to 2 weeks.

Makes 2 pints

Poor Man's Capers

*N*ASTURTIUMS ARE MY FAVORITE FLOWERS. WHERE I LIVE THEY FLOURISH AND BLOOM FOR ONLY A BRIEF TIME IN SPRING. THUS, I MUST NURSE THE PLANTS THROUGH THE DRY SUMMER HEAT AND THE WINTER FREEZES SO THAT, COME SPRING, THEY WILL AGAIN SPILL OVER THE EDGE OF THEIR BED. THEY COVER MY BRICK PATIO WITH THEIR HUGE FLAT GREEN LEAVES, AND SEND UP LONG, SUCCULENT STEMS TO BEAR MAHOGANY, CRIMSON, GOLD, AND YELLOW FLOWERS THAT TASTE LIKE PEPPERED HONEY. THE VINES CLIMB UP AND OUT, COVERING THE OLD WOODEN WALLS OF THE OUTBUILDINGS, WHILE THE FLOWERS AND LEAVES MAKE COLUMNS OF COLOR ALONG THEIR SPRAWLING LENGTHS.

ONE MORE REASON TO FAVOR THESE VERSATILE FLOWERS IS THAT THE PLUMP, ROUND IMMATURE NASTURTIUM SEEDPODS TASTE LIKE CAPERS WHEN PICKLED. TRUE CAPERS COME FROM CAPPARIS SPINOSA A BUSH THAT THRIVES IN MEDITERRANEAN CLIMATES.

◆

6 cups water
1³/₄ cups salt
1 cup immature nasturtium seedpods
2 cups red wine vinegar

◆

In a nonreactive saucepan over high heat, combine the water and 1½ cups of the salt to make a brine. Bring to a boil and boil, stirring, until the salt dissolves, 3 or 4 minutes. Remove from the heat and let cool to room temperature.

Clean any bits of dirt or leaves from the seedpods, then wash them and drain well. Put one-third of the brine in a glass bowl; reserve the remaining brine in a covered jar. Add the nasturtium pods and let stand overnight.

The next day, drain the nasturtium pods. Using the reserved brine, repeat the soaking of the nasturtium pods twice. When the pods are drained on the third day, combine the vinegar and the remaining ¼ cup salt in a nonreactive saucepan over high heat. Bring to a boil and boil, stirring, until the salt dissolves, 2 to 3 minutes.

Loosely pack the nasturtium pods into small, hot, dry, sterilized jars with lids. Pour in the hot vinegar to within ½ inch of the rims and cover with the lids.

Store the jars in a cool, dark place or in the refrigerator. The "capers" will keep for up to 3 months.

Makes about a ½ pint

Rhubarb Chutney

*T*HE MENTION OF RHUBARB ELICITS EITHER ENTHUSIASTIC CHILDHOOD RECOLLEC-
TIONS OF THE TART TASTE OF HOMEMADE RHUBARB PIES AND PRESERVES OR THE PUZZLED
INQUIRY OF, "WHAT DO YOU DO WITH IT?" RHUBARB'S TANGY, ACIDIC TASTE MAKES IT IDEAL
FOR CHUTNEY, WHICH REQUIRES A BALANCE BETWEEN SHARP AND SWEET. UNFORTUNATELY,
THE PINK-ROSE HUE OF THE STALKS IS LOST WHEN THEY ARE COOKED WITH BROWN SUGAR
AND SPICES, SO THE RESULTING CHUTNEY IS NOT PINK BUT A RICH, DEEP BROWN. THIS PAR-
TICULAR CHUTNEY IS DELICIOUS EATEN WITH A CHUNK OF CHEDDAR CHEESE AND A THICK
SLICE OF BREAD.

◆

5 or 6 rhubarb stalks
2 cups firmly packed brown sugar
1 cup cider vinegar
1 tablespoon chopped lemon zest
1 cinnamon stick,
about 4 inches long
1-inch-piece fresh ginger,
peeled and minced
1 cup golden raisins
1/4 teaspoon salt
1 cup coarsely chopped walnuts

◆

Trim the rhubarb stalks
and cut into pieces
1 inch thick. You will
need 3½ to 4 cups
pieces. Set aside.

Combine the sugar,
vinegar, and lemon zest
in a stainless-steel or
other nonreactive sauce-
pan and cook over low
heat, stirring, until the
sugar dissolves, 5 or 6
minutes. Add the rhu-
barb, cinnamon stick,
and ginger, raise the heat
to medium, and cook,
stirring frequently, until
the rhubarb is soft, about
15 minutes. Add the
raisins, salt, and walnuts.
Cook for another 3 to 4
minutes.

Ladle the chutney
into clean, dry jars with
sealable lids, filling the
jars to within ½ inch of
the rims. Using a damp
cloth, wipe the rims
clean. Cover with the
lids and process for 30
minutes in a hot-water
bath (see instructions for
processing hot-pack
foods on page 21).

Remove the jars
and let them cool for
12 hours or overnight.
Check the lids for a
complete seal.

Store the sealed jars
in a cool, dark place.
The chutney will keep
for up to 1 year. Once
opened, keep refriger-
ated. Store any jar

lacking a good seal in
the refrigerator for up to
3 weeks.

Alternatively, do not
process the chutney in a
water bath. Simply ladle
into dry, sterilized jars,
cover with lids, and store
in the refrigerator for up
to 3 weeks.

Makes about 2 pints

From left to right:
Pickled Artichokes
Tarragon Vinegar
Wild Greens and Garlic Relish
Brandied Cherries
Green Herb Mustard
Poor Man's Capers
Candied Rose Petals
Rhubarb Chutney

Sweet-and-Sour Radishes

*T*HIS IS AN UNCOMPLICATED WAY TO SHOW OFF THE BRILLIANT SCARLET AND PURE WHITE OF GARDEN-FRESH SPRING RADISHES. BECAUSE THE LEAVES ARE AS CRISP AND TENDER AS THE RADISHES THEMSELVES, LEAVE A FEW OF THEM ATTACHED WHEN YOU PREPARE THIS EARLY SEASON DISH. I SERVE THESE RADISHES AS AN HORS D'OEUVRE AND AS AN ACCOMPANIMENT TO GRILLED OR ROASTED MEATS.

◆

30 small radishes with leaves intact (3 to 4 bunches)

1 teaspoon salt

1 tablespoon soy sauce

2 tablespoons rice wine vinegar or distilled white vinegar

1 teaspoon dry sherry

1 teaspoon granulated sugar

2 tablespoons Asian sesame oil

1 tablespoon water

1 teaspoon sesame seeds, lightly toasted (optional)

◆

Remove any large or discolored leaves from the radishes, leaving intact several of the perfect young leaves. Using the back of a wooden spoon or a small mallet, hit each radish just hard enough to break it open slightly but not so hard that it is crushed. Put the radishes in a shallow glass bowl or dish and sprinkle with the salt. Let stand for 10 to 15 minutes.

In a small bowl stir together the soy sauce, vinegar, sherry, sugar, sesame oil, water, and sesame seeds (if using). Pour the mixture over the radishes. Turn the radishes gently in the sauce and let them stand for at least 20 minutes before serving.

The radishes and their sauce can also be packed into dry, sterilized jars, covered, and refrigerated. They will keep for up to 1 week.

Makes about 1½ pints

Green Herb Mustard

SHARP, TANGY SPRING HERBS AND GREENS SUCH AS YOUNG SORREL, ARUGULA, AND CHIVES FLAVOR THIS HOT MUSTARD. JUST SMELLING IT MAKES ME WANT TO EAT SAUSAGES! THIS MUSTARD IS AROMATIC AND HOT, AND IT DRAWS ITS INSPIRATION FROM THE WHITE WINE MUSTARDS FOR WHICH DIJON IS FAMOUS. WHETHER SPREAD ON THICK, CHEWY PRETZELS OR BLENDED INTO A VINAIGRETTE SAUCE, THIS HERB-LACED BLEND CARRIES THE TASTE OF SPRING.

◆

1/2 teaspoon salt

1 teaspoon granulated sugar

1/2 teaspoon white pepper

1/2 cup white wine vinegar

2 cups water

1 cup dry mustard

1/2 cup minced mixed young fresh herbs and greens, such as sorrel, chives, arugula, chervil, and tarragon

◆

Combine the salt, sugar, pepper, vinegar, and water in a stainless-steel or other nonreactive frying pan or saucepan and bring to a boil over high heat. Slowly stir in the dry mustard. Reduce the heat to low and simmer until the mixture thickens to a creamy consistency, stirring occasionally at first and then more frequently as it thickens, about 1 hour.

Stir in the herbs and simmer for 1 to 2 minutes. Remove from the heat and spoon into hot, dry, sterilized jars with lids. Cover tightly and store in the refrigerator. The mustard will keep for up to 3 months.

Makes about 1 pint

Tarragon or Chervil Vinegar

TARRAGON AND CHERVIL ARE MY FIRST SPRING HERBS, WITH SPRIGHTLY GREEN LEAVES BRIGHTENING THE GARDEN AND BRINGING A FRESH, SHARP TASTE TO THE KITCHEN AFTER WINTER'S DEARTH. CHERVIL'S FAINT HINT OF LICORICE AND TARRAGON'S SWEET CITRUS TASTE ARE BOTH EASILY CAPTURED AND PRESERVED IN VINEGAR. FISH AND VEGETABLE DISHES ARE ESPECIALLY ENHANCED BY THESE DELICATE SPRING VINEGARS.

◆

1 cup firmly packed
fresh tarragon or chervil sprigs
4 cups white wine vinegar

◆

Put the tarragon or chervil sprigs into a dry, sterilized widemouthed jar with a lid. Pour in the vinegar and cover with the lid. Place the jar in a sunny location, indoors or outside, and let stand for about 10 days or until the vinegar has become infused with the flavor of the herbs to your satisfaction.

Strain the vinegar through a sieve lined with several layers of cheesecloth; discard the herbs. Decant into dry, sterilized bottles. A fresh sprig of tarragon or chervil may be added for decoration, but after a few weeks it may begin to deteriorate. Seal with corks and store the bottles in a cool, dark place. The vinegar will keep for up to 1 year.

Makes 2 pints

Vin de Cerise

PITTED RIPE CHERRIES SOAKED IN A
SWEETENED, FORTIFIED RED WINE RESULT IN A
PLEASANT VIN DE MAISON APERITIF WINE THAT IS
EQUALLY GOOD SERVED OVER ICE IN SUMMER OR
AT COOL ROOM TEMPERATURE IN WINTER. THE
WINE-SOAKED CHERRIES ARE REMOVED AFTER TWO
DAYS AND, IN A TRIUMPH OF RECYCLING, THEY
CAN BE BAKED IN A CUSTARDY CLAFOUTI.

◆

*1 pound sweet
or sour ripe cherries
1 fifth dry red wine
1¹/₂ cups confectioners' sugar
¹/₄ cup kirsch*

◆

Discard any blemished cherries. Stem and pit the cherries as described in Whole Cherry Preserves (page 31). Combine the pitted cherries, wine, and sugar in a large, stainless-steel or other nonreactive saucepan and bring the mixture to a gentle boil over medium-high heat. Cook for 5 minutes.

Transfer the mixture to a hot, dry, sterilized jar or crock with a wide mouth. Add the kirsch, cover, and let stand in a cool, dark place for 2 days.

Remove the cherries and, if you wish, use them in any dish calling for macerated cherries. Filter the wine into a dry, sterilized bottle, pouring it through a funnel lined with several layers of cheesecloth. Cork the bottle and store the wine in a cool, dark place. It will keep for up to 1 year.

Makes about 1 fifth

Brandied Cherries

When jars of these cherries have stood awhile, the perfect deep rose spheres press against the glass walls, suspended in brandy that has turned maroon, and the fine, threadlike stems can be seen faintly crisscrossing.

At the turn of the century in the gilded rooms of fine hotels in Europe and America, waiters wheeled in towers of flaming brandied cherries. Although such a presentation may seem too overpowering, too rich for today's taste, the cachet of brandied cherries remains, making them an elegant gift to give or to receive. For quieter occasions, spoon them over ice cream or cake, or serve them, a few stems at a time, in a liqueur glass along with the flavored brandy.

Either sweet cherries, such as the popular Bing variety, or the sour Montmorency or Morello, my personal favorites, can be used.

◆

4 pounds ripe cherries,
preferably with stems
1 cup granulated sugar
1/4 cup water
4 cups brandy

◆

Discard any blemished cherries. Stem and pit one-fourth of the cherries as described in Whole Cherry Preserves (page 31). Put the pulp and pits in a stainless-steel or other nonreactive saucepan. Add the sugar and water and bring to a simmer over medium heat. Reduce the heat and cook slowly until a thick syrup forms, about 15 minutes. Remove from the heat and scoop out and discard the pits.

Put the remaining whole cherries in a dry, sterilized jar with a lid large enough to hold all the cherries, the syrup, and the brandy. Stir together the cherry syrup and brandy and pour the mixture over the cherries. Cover with the lid.

Store in a cool, dark place for 1 month before using the cherries. The cherries, along with some of the flavored brandy, can be put into smaller dry, sterilized jars at this time, if you wish. Continue to store the cherries in a cool, dark place. The cherries will keep for up to 1 year.

Makes about 2 quarts

Dried Apricots

*S*HOULD YOU BE FORTUNATE TO HAVE AN ABUNDANCE OF APRICOTS, CONSIDER DRYING THEM. THE ONES THAT ARE A BIT OVERRIPE AND SOFT TO THE TOUCH GENERALLY HAVE A HIGHER SUGAR CONTENT, RESULTING IN A DRIED FRUIT SO SWEET IT CAN BE GIVEN AS A GIFT IN PLACE OF CANDY.

◆

24 very ripe apricots
(about 5 pounds)

◆

Slit the apricots open lengthwise and remove and discard the pits. (Although you may dry pitted whole apricots, they will dry more quickly if halved.)

For successful outdoor drying, the fruits must be exposed to warm, circulating air. Commercial processors dry apricots on wooden racks, but a plastic screen or tautly stretched netting works equally well. Arrange the apricot halves in a single layer and turn them once or twice each day. If evenings and mornings are dew-laden, gather the drying fruits into a protected area overnight. The apricots will darken as they dry and are ready when they are chewy but no longer juicy. This may take 4 or 5 days under normal conditions, and longer in cooler or moister climates.

Pack the dried apricots in a tin, glass jar, or box with a lid and store in a cool, dry place. The apricots will keep for up to 1 year.

Makes 48 apricot halves

Candied Rose Petals

I AM PERPETUALLY FASCINATED BY CAKES DECORATED WITH SWIRLS OF SPUN SUGAR AND PYRAMIDS OF DELICATELY FORMED FLOWERS AND LEAVES. UNFORTUNATELY, I HAVE A LONG RECORD OF FAILING TO CREATE THESE WORKS OF ART. CONSEQUENTLY, I HAVE MASTERED THE UNCOMPLICATED SKILL OF SUGARING NATURE'S CREATIONS. ROSE PETALS ARE EASY TO CANDY BECAUSE THEY ARE FLAT, BUT THE SAME TECHNIQUE CAN BE APPLIED TO WHOLE FLOWERS SUCH AS VIOLETS, ROSEBUDS, PANSIES, NASTURTIUMS, OR ANY OTHER EDIBLE BLOSSOMS.

IF YOU HAVE THE PATIENCE TO KEEP THE CANDIED PETALS UNTIL WINTER, THE BRIGHT HUES OF SPRING'S VELVET REDS, PINKS, AND YELLOWS STREWN ACROSS A CAKE OR CUPCAKES MAKE MAGNIFICENT REMINDERS OF SPRING'S GENTLE SEASON.

◆

24 unbruised,
pesticide-free fresh rose petals
3 egg whites
1 cup superfine sugar

◆

Place the egg whites in a bowl and, using a fork or whisk, beat until frothy but not stiff. Lay the rose petals in a layer on a sheet of waxed paper. Put the sugar in a bowl.

Using a small paint brush, paint each petal on both sides with the egg whites, then put the petal in the bowl of sugar and spoon more sugar over it. Using tweezers carefully lift up the petal and shake off the excess sugar. Return the petal to the paper to dry. Repeat the process until all the petals are sugared. If the egg whites begin to lose their frothiness, beat them again. Let the candied rose petals dry overnight.

Once the petals are thoroughly dry, pack them into a tin, glass jar, or paper bag. Store in a cool, dry place. The petals will keep for up to 6 months or longer.

Makes 24 sugared petals

SUMMER

◆

Plum Jam

Rose Geranium Jelly

Watermelon Rind Preserves

Fresh Herb and Vegetable Relish

Grilled Eggplant Layered with

Shaved Garlic and Fresh Thyme

Summer Antipasto

Italian Whole Roast Peppers

in Herbed Olive Oil

Gold or Red Pickled Beets,

Italian Style

Pickled Baby Corn

Brined Grape Leaves

Nectarine Mustard

Yellow Tomato Ketchup

Green or Purple Basil Vinegars

Lavender Syrup

Dried Tomatoes

◆

In the Summer . . .

Summer, the season of abundance, is the ultimate canning season. In the past when there were no supermarkets and long-distance, year-round shipping of perishable foods was in its infancy, enough fruits and vegetables were "put up" by a family during the summer to last until the next summer. This was tremendously laborious work that usually fell to the women and children. ✦ Today, preserving summer fruits and vegetables is done more for the enjoyment of the task and the beauty and taste of the end product than out of necessity. Come the maturing of dark purple eggplants and brilliant Corno di Toro peppers in my garden, I look forward to the moment when I will capture them, in all their summer essence, into savory treats laden with garlic, vinegar, herbs, and olive oil, to serve when winter's rains are falling. ✦ Drying tomatoes of all different colors and sizes is another of my special summer projects, along with pickling baby corn. Because the fresh sweet corn readily available at farmer's markets is so delicious, I no longer grow corn at home, other than miniature corn for pickling. Seeing the tiny ears, with their perfectly formed kernels visible through the walls of clear jars, is sufficient reason to make them. More practically speaking, they are fine accompaniments to pâtés and to salads of all kinds. ✦ Summer's garden is full of pungent purple and green basil plants, so I continuously infuse vinegar with their harvest. I use the vinegar regularly for deglazing skillets of onion confit or caramelized sweet potatoes because of the unusual perfume summer's basil imparts to the finished dish. Wrapped with exotic ribbons and papers, the flavored vinegars make special gifts anytime of the year. ✦ For me, the most exotic of all summer's special preserves is rose geranium jelly. I put up only a few jars—I don't want to decimate my beautiful rose geranium plant—and only very reluctantly put the finished jars away in the basement, preferring to look at the light shining through the pale jelly sitting on my windowsill. ✦ Generally, I would rather eat summer's ripe fruits fresh from the trees and vines than to preserve them, but there are a few exceptions. Plum jam practically makes itself, which puts it high on my list of summer cooking, while a few jars of watermelon rind preserves are needed throughout the year for eating with curries and other spicy dishes. ✦ Summer preserving, like fall preserving, is highly personal because there is so much from which to choose. No single fruit or vegetable dominates the summer season as cherries and apricots do the spring or citrus fruits do the winter.

Plum Jam

ONE OF THE MOST REWARDING OF ALL JAMS, PLUM JAM IS EASY TO PREPARE, COLOR-
FUL, AND HAS A SATISFYING TASTE. SWEET, OF COURSE, BUT RETAINING ITS TART INTEGRITY
NEVERTHELESS, PLUM JAM CAN BE MADE IN AT LEAST A HALF-DOZEN DIFFERENT COLORS, EACH
ONE WITH A DISTINCTIVE FLAVOR. TINY WILD PLUMS MAKE A PALE PINK OR DELICATE YELLOW
JAM, DEPENDING UPON WHICH KIND YOU USE, AND THE STURDY ELEPHANT HEART VARIETY
YIELDS JARS OF DEEP RED. THE DIFFICULT-TO-FIND BLUE DAMSON PLUM, CONSIDERED BY MANY
TO MAKE THE FINEST OF ALL PLUM JAMS, TURNS A REGAL PURPLE WHEN IT IS COOKED.

◆

2$^1/_2$ pounds firm,
slightly underripe plums
3$^1/_2$ cups granulated sugar

◆

Pit the plums, then chop them into fine bits to measure approximately 4 cups. Put the chopped fruit into a large, stainless-steel or other non-reactive saucepan and stir in the sugar. Let the mixture stand for 1 hour or so.

Over medium heat, bring the mixture slowly to a boil, stirring often. Cook rapidly, stirring often, for about 15 minutes, then begin to test for the jell point (see instructions on page 22). Alternatively, insert a candy thermometer in the mixture. When it reads 220 degrees F, the jam is ready.

Remove from the heat. Skim off and discard any surface foam. Ladle the jam into hot, dry, sterilized jars, filling to within ¼ inch of the rim. Seal with a ⅛-inch-thick layer of melted paraffin (see directions for working with paraffin on page 22).

Allow that layer to harden, then add a second layer of the same thickness. Using a damp cloth, wipe the rims clean. Cover with lids, aluminum foil, or with waxed paper or cotton cloth tightly fastened with twine or a rubber band.

Store in a cool, dark place. The jam will keep for up to 1 year.

Makes about 2 pints

Rose Geranium Jelly

Half the pleasure of making this jelly is the fun of using an ingredient as exotic as scented geranium leaves. Plucking the intensely perfumed leaves from the decorative potted plant that sits in my dining room window, then packing them into an ordinary measuring cup seems steps removed from the practical process of turning fruits into jelly and more akin to a child's game of making secret potions. The infusion made from steeping the leaves imparts a lingering, slightly mysterious flavor that becomes discernible a moment after swallowing—much like a surprising finish on a memorable wine.

The unripe apples provide natural pectin for the jelling, but contribute surprisingly little to the taste. If you cannot find unripe green apples, substitute tart green cooking apples.

2 cups loosely packed
fresh rose geranium leaves
6 cups water
8 small or 6 medium-size
unripe apples or tart green apples,
such as Granny Smith
3 cups granulated sugar

Put the geranium leaves in a glass bowl. Bring 4 cups of the water to a boil. Pour the boiling water over the leaves and let steep overnight to create an infusion.

The next day, core and stem the apples but do not peel. Chop into 1-inch chunks. You will have about 2 cups. Put the remaining 2 cups water in a saucepan, add the apples, and place over low heat. Cook the apples until they are mushy, 15 to 20 minutes.

Remove the apple mixture from the heat and press it through a food mill or a fine-mesh strainer placed over a bowl. The result will be a bowl of pale green pulp, with the peels remaining behind in the mill or strainer. Discard the peels.

Rinse a jelly bag with water, wring it out well, and hang the bag over a large bowl. Transfer the pulp to the jelly bag. Remove and discard the geranium leaves from the infusion and add the infusion to the jelly bag. Leave the mixture to drip. It will take about 2 hours for the liquid to drip through the bag completely.

There will be approximately 4 cups liquid.

Pour the liquid into a stainless-steel or other nonreactive saucepan and add the sugar. Place over medium-low heat and stir to dissolve the sugar. Continue to cook, stirring often, for about 30 minutes, then begin to test for the jell point (see instructions on page 22). Alternatively, insert a candy thermometer in the mixture. When it reads 220 degrees F, the jelly is ready.

Remove from the heat. Skim off and discard any surface foam. Ladle the jelly into hot, dry, sterilized jars, filling to within ¼ inch of the rims. Seal with a ⅛-inch-thick layer of melted paraffin (see directions for working with paraffin page 22). Allow that layer to harden, then add a second layer of the same thickness. Using a damp cloth, wipe the rims clean. Cover with lids, aluminum foil, or with waxed paper or cotton cloth tightly fastened with twine or a rubber band.

Store in a cool, dark place. The jelly will keep for up to 1 year.

Makes 2 pints

Watermelon Rind Preserves

Every year of my childhood my grandmother made these thick preserves, and every year I disdained them. Later, as an adult, I discovered they were a perfect condiment for East Indian curries, along with yogurt and chopped fresh cilantro and tarragon leaves.

The texture of these preserves is firm and the taste is of clove and cinnamon. The most suitable melon, if you can get it, is the old-fashioned citron melon, with its solid three- to four-inch-thick rind. Since these melons are hard to come by, a good substitute is an underripe watermelon with a thick rind.

◆

1 pound watermelon rind

5 quarts water

$1/2$ cup salt

2 cups granulated sugar

1 lemon, sliced

1 cinnamon stick,
about 2 inches long

1 teaspoon whole cloves

◆

Peel the skin from the rind and scrape the rind clean of any flesh. Cut the rind into ½-inch cubes. Combine 4 quarts of the water and the salt in a large bowl and stir to dissolve the salt. Add the rind and let soak overnight at room temperature.

The next day, drain the rind. Place it in a stainless-steel or other nonreactive saucepan with 2 cups of the remaining water and bring to a boil over high heat. Lower the heat and simmer until the rind is just tender when pierced with a fork, about 50 minutes. Drain well and set aside.

In a saucepan large enough to hold the rind eventually, combine all the remaining ingredients, including the remaining 2 cups water. Bring slowly to a boil, stirring to dissolve the sugar. Boil until the sugar dissolves and a syrup forms, about 5 minutes. Add the rind and cook over low heat until it becomes transparent, about 30 minutes.

Using a slotted utensil, remove the rind pieces and pack them tightly into hot, clean, dry jars with sealable lids. Ladle the hot syrup into the jars, filling the jars to within ½ inch of the rims. Using a damp cloth, wipe the rims clean. Cover with the lids and process for 30 minutes in a hot-water bath (see instructions for processing hot-pack foods on page 21).

Remove the jars and let them cool 12 hours or overnight. Check for a complete seal.

Store the sealed jars in a cool, dark place. The preserves will keep for up to 1 year. Once opened, keep refrigerated. Store any jar lacking a good seal in the refrigerator for up to 2 weeks.

Makes 2 to 3 pints

Fresh Herb and Vegetable Relish

THIS IS ONE OF THE MOST FLAVORFUL RELISHES I KNOW. THE DISTINCTIVE TASTES OF THE FRESH HERBS INTERMINGLE AND BLEND WITH THOSE OF THE CRUNCHY, FINELY DICED VEGETABLES, AS ALL OF THE INGREDIENTS STEEP TOGETHER IN THE BRINE. A VERSATILE RELISH, IT MAY BE SPREAD ON SANDWICHES OR SERVED AS A SPICY SIDE DISH TO CLASSICALLY SIMPLE MEAT DISHES SUCH AS ITALIAN bollito misto.

◆

1/4 cup finely diced cabbage
2 cups finely diced,
peeled cucumber
1 cup finely diced onion
1 1/2 cups finely diced fennel
1/4 cup finely diced garlic
1 cup finely diced red
or green sweet pepper
1 cup finely diced celery
1 1/4 cups finely minced
mixed fresh parsley, mint,
tarragon, basil, and chives,
in any ratio
2 tablespoons salt
6 cups red wine vinegar

◆

Combine all of the ingredients in a large glass bowl. Cover and refrigerate for 4 days.

Using a slotted utensil, remove the vegetables from the bowl, reserving the vinegar, and snugly pack them into dry, sterilized jars with lids to within ½ inch of the rims. Pour in enough of the vinegar to cover the vegetables completely. Cover with the lids.

The relish will keep in the refrigerator for up to 3 months.

Makes about 3 pints

Grilled Eggplant Layered with Shaved Garlic and Fresh Thyme

*T*HIS IS A GARLIC LOVER'S DELIGHT. SHAVINGS OF GARLIC AND THYME ARE CAPTURED BETWEEN SEASONED LAYERS OF CRISPY, GOLDEN EGGPLANT STRIPS, AND THEN A MIXTURE OF OLIVE OIL AND RED WINE VINEGAR IS POURED OVER THE TOP. AFTER A WEEK, THE EGGPLANT, INFUSED WITH THE FLAVOR OF THE THYME AND GARLIC, WILL HAVE ABSORBED THE OLIVE OIL AND VINEGAR. A FAVORITE EXTRAVAGANT USE FOR THESE PRESERVES IS TO ARRANGE THEM ON A SLICE OF TOASTED FOCACCIA AND TOP THEM WITH ROASTED SWEET PEPPERS (SEE PAGE 67), A FEW FRESH HERBS, AND A SECOND SLICE OF TOASTED FOCACCIA. LEAH BERGEN, A SAN FRANCISCO BAY AREA CHEF, FIRST SHARED THIS RECIPE WITH ME.

◆

4 eggplants,
about ¹/₂ pound each
³/₄ to 1 cup olive oil
2 tablespoons salt
2 tablespoons freshly ground
black pepper
6 garlic cloves, sliced paper-thin
6 tablespoons chopped
fresh thyme, marjoram, or oregano
¹/₂ to ¹/₃ cup balsamic vinegar

◆

Prepare a fire in a charcoal grill or preheat a broiler. Cut the eggplants lengthwise into slices ⅜ inch thick. Cut these slices into long strips 1 inch wide. Brush the strips with 3 to 4 tablespoons of the olive oil and arrange them on a grill rack or broiler tray. Grill or broil them, turning once, until golden, 3 to 5 minutes on each side. Remove and set aside until cool enough to handle, about 10 minutes.

Arrange a layer of eggplant in the bottom of a dry, sterilized wide-mouthed 1-quart jar with a lid. Sprinkle with some of the salt, pepper, garlic, and thyme. Continue layering in the same manner until all of the eggplant, garlic, and thyme have been used. Combine the remaining olive oil and the vinegar and pour it over the eggplant layers. Cover with the lid.

Place in the refrigerator. Turn the jar upside down every other day for a week to allow the liquid to penetrate all the layers. At the end of the week, the eggplant will be ready to eat, but the flavor will continue to develop with age. Store in the refrigerator for up to 6 months.

Makes 1 quart

From left to right:
Lavender Syrup
Grilled Eggplant Layered
with Shaved Garlic
and Fresh Thyme
Plum Jam
Fresh Herb and Vegetable Relish
Rose Geranium Jelly
Watermelon Rind Preserves
Purple Basil Vinegar
Nectarine Mustard

Summer Antipasto

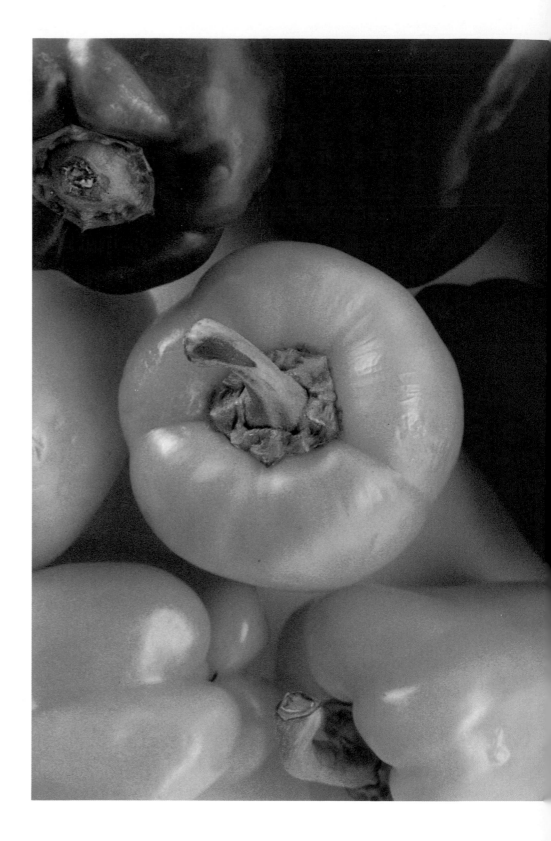

*M*OST READILY AVAILABLE COMMER-
CIAL ITALIAN ANTIPASTO MIXTURES ARE ASSEM-
BLAGES OF WINTER VEGETABLES—CAULIFLOWER,
CELERY, CARROTS—BUT THIS FARMHOUSE VER-
SION IS MADE WITH THE EGGPLANTS, BASIL, AND
COLORFUL SWEET PEPPERS OF SUMMER.

THE VEGETABLES SLICES, FIRST BLANCHED
IN VINEGAR, ARE ARRANGED IN JARS IN LAYERS
STUDDED WITH OLIVE SLICES; LARGE PURPLE AND
GREEN BASIL LEAVES ARE PRESSED AGAINST THE
JAR SIDES. FINALLY, ANY LITTLE EMPTY SPACES
THAT REMAIN ARE FLOODED WITH OLIVE OIL, THEN
THE PACKED JAR IS PROCESSED IN A HOT-WATER
BATH.

IF YOU ARE A LOVER OF SALTY TASTES, ADD
A FEW ANCHOVY FILLETS ALONG WITH THE OLIVES.

◆

2¹/₂ pounds sweet peppers,
a mixture of yellow, orange, red,
and gold or any other combination
2¹/₂ pounds eggplant
5 cups white wine vinegar
6 to 8 whole cloves
2 tablespoons black peppercorns
¹/₂ cup coarsely chopped
fresh parsley
2 teaspoons salt
20 fresh green or purple
basil leaves, or a mixture
4 ounces pitted large green olives,
sliced (about 1 cup)
About 1¹/₄ cups good-quality,
fruity olive oil

◆

Cut the sweet peppers in half lengthwise. Remove and discard the stems, seeds, and ribs. Cut the peppers into long strips about ½ inch wide and set aside.

Remove the stems from the eggplants. If you are using long, slender Japanese eggplants, cut lengthwise into slices ½ inch thick. If you are using globular eggplants, first cut them crosswise into ½-inch-thick rounds, then cut each round into ½-inch-wide strips. Set aside.

In a stainless-steel or other nonreactive saucepan, combine the vinegar, cloves, and 1 tablespoon of the peppercorns and bring to a boil over high heat. Add the pepper strips, reduce the heat to medium, and simmer for 2 to 3 minutes. Using a slotted utensil, remove the pepper from the vinegar and set them aside. Add the eggplants to the vinegar and simmer in the same manner. Remove the eggplants, as well.

Have ready clean, dry jars with sealable lids. Arrange a layer of eggplant strips in a jar. Top with a layer of pepper strips and sprinkle with a little of the parsley and salt and 1 or 2 peppercorns. Then press a basil leaf against the wall of the jar, scatter a few olive slices on top, and pour in about 2 tablespoons of the olive oil. Repeat this layering process until the jars are full. Lastly, add olive oil to the jars to cover the contents completely and to reach to within ½ inch of the jar rims. Using a damp cloth, wipe the rims clean. Cover with the lids and process for 30 minutes in a hot-water bath (see instructions for processing cold-pack foods on page 21).

Remove the jars and let them cool for 12 hours or overnight. Check the lids for a complete seal. Store the sealed jars in a cool, dark place.

The antipasto will keep for up to 1 year. Once opened, keep refrigerated. Store any jar lacking a good seal in the refrigerator for up to 2 weeks.

Makes about 3 pints

Italian Whole Roast Peppers in Herbed Olive Oil

You have likely seen commercial versions of these peppers dramatically displayed in Italian delicatessens, here or in Italy, where tier after tier of red and yellow sweet peppers are packed in huge decorative jars that perch on counters or shelves.

At home, you can put up equally huge amounts of peppers, packing them into your own jars, or you can prepare just a few peppers to have on hand for appetizers, to tuck into special sandwiches, or to eat alongside meats and vegetables.

The classic Corno di Toro, the Bull's Horn pepper, is used in this preparation, but any other large sweet pepper will make a good substitute. The peppers are first roasted, then soaked overnight in a mixture of vinegar and salt. On the following day, they are drained and packed in fruity olive oil, along with a few sprigs of rosemary, some bay leaves, and a few peppercorns.

◆

3 pounds sweet peppers,
a mixture of red and yellow
1 tablespoon salt
3 cups white wine vinegar
6 cloves garlic
9 fresh or dried bay leaves
6 fresh rosemary sprigs
2 tablespoons black peppercorns
About 3 cups good-quality,
fruity olive oil

◆

Preheat an oven to 500 degrees F or preheat a broiler, or prepare a fire in a charcoal grill. Arrange the peppers in a shallow pan, on a broiler tray, or on a grill rack, and roast or grill, turning to color evenly, until blackened on all sides, 3 to 4 minutes per side. Slip the peppers into a plastic bag and close the top. Let stand to allow the skins to steam and loosen, 4 to 5 minutes.

Remove the peppers from the bag and slip off the blackened skins. Gently pull or cut out the stems. Make a single lengthwise slit in each pepper and remove the seeds. Rinse and pat dry.

In a small, nonreactive saucepan, combine the salt and vinegar and bring to a boil over high heat. Meanwhile, put the roasted peppers in a clean, dry stainless-steel, glass, or ceramic bowl or in a jar. Pour in the hot vinegar to cover and top with plastic wrap, a lid, or other cover. Let stand overnight at room temperature.

The next day, drain off the vinegar and remove the peppers from the bowl or jar. Pat the peppers dry with paper or cloth towels. Pack them into dry, sterilized jars, forming alternate layers of red and yellow peppers and tucking in the garlic cloves, bay leaves, rosemary sprigs, and peppercorns as you do. Pour in the olive oil to cover; as you add the oil, slide a knife between the peppers and the jar sides to break any air pockets and to make sure the oil penetrates fully.

Top with tight-fitting lids. Store in a cool, dark place for 1 week.

At the end of that week, retrieve and discard the garlic cloves, then store the peppers in the refrigerator. They will keep for up to 3 months.

Makes 3 pints

Gold or Red Pickled Beets, Italian Style

*H*ERE, SMALL GOLD OR RED BEETS WITH A FEW OF THEIR YOUNG LEAVES LEFT
INTACT ARE COOKED UNTIL TENDER, THEN COVERED WITH A WELL-SPICED PICKLING BRINE THAT
INCLUDES JUNIPER BERRIES, FRESH OREGANO, AND LEAFY CELERY STALKS. WHETHER SERVED
AS PART OF A CLASSIC ANTIPASTO OR ALONG WITH A PLATTER OF TURKEY OR HAM, THIS ITAL-
IAN FARMHOUSE PICKLE HAS THE TASTE OF A COUNTRY GARDEN.

IF ONLY LARGE BEETS ARE AVAILABLE, YOU WILL NEED ABOUT HALF AS MANY BEETS.
THEY MUST ALSO COOK LONGER, PERHAPS AS LONG AS AN HOUR. ONCE THEY ARE PEELED, CUT
THEM INTO QUARTERS LENGTHWISE BEFORE PACKING INTO JARS.

◆

24 small gold or red beets,
1 to 2 inches in diameter,
with tops intact
4 teaspoons salt
1 1/3 cups white wine vinegar,
for gold beets, or red
wine vinegar, for red beets
2 fresh or dried bay leaves
2 small onions, unpeeled
4 small celery stalks,
cut into 2- to 3-inch pieces,
with leaves
1 cinnamon stick,
about 2 inches long
3 or 4 juniper berries
3 whole cloves
6 black peppercorns
2 fresh oregano sprigs,
each about 3 inches long
1/4 cup granulated sugar
6 to 8 beet leaves (optional)

◆

Trim the tops of the beets carefully, removing the large leaves but leaving the small leaves— 1/2 inch to 1 inch long— attached. Set aside 6 to 8 of the nicest large leaves, if desired.

Put the beets in a saucepan and add water to cover and 2 teaspoons of the salt. Bring the water to a boil and boil the beets just until tender when pierced with a knife tip, 15 to 20 minutes.

Remove the saucepan from the heat and drain the beets. As soon as

they are cool enough to handle, peel them, using your fingers to slip the skins off. Try not to slough off the little leaves along with the skin. The skin of barely done beets is a little more difficult to remove, but the leaves are more likely to remain attached than those on fully done beets. If you wish, cut the larger of the cooked young beets in half, but leave the smaller ones whole. Let cool to room temperature.

To prepare the brine, combine all the remaining ingredients, includ-ing the remaining 2 teaspoons salt and the

6 to 8 beet leaves (if using), in a stainless-steel or other nonreactive saucepan and bring to a boil over high heat. Reduce the heat to medium and simmer for 5 minutes. Remove from the heat and let cool completely to room temperature.

Using a slotted utensil, pack the cooked beets snugly into clean, dry jars with sealable lids. Remove the whole onions from the brine and discard them. Pour the cooled brine over the beets, filling the jars to within 1/2 inch of the rims. Using a damp

cloth, wipe the rims clean. Cover with the lids and process for 30 minutes in a hot-water bath (see instructions for processing cold-pack foods on page 21).

Remove the jars and let them cool for 12 hours or overnight. Check the lids for a complete seal. Store the sealed jars in a cool, dark place.

The beets will keep for up to 1 year. Once opened, keep refriger-ated. Store any jar lacking a good seal in the refrigerator for up to 2 weeks.

Makes 2 pints

Pickled Baby Corn

*T*HIS IS A SHORT-CUT METHOD
FOR PICKLING BABY CORN THAT GIVES RESULTS
IN HOURS RATHER THAN WEEKS.

◆

1 cup water

1 cup white wine vinegar

2 cloves garlic

½ teaspoon granulated sugar

2 whole cloves

1 teaspoon salt

1 large fresh tarragon sprig,

or 1 tablespoon

fresh tarragon leaves

36 ears baby corn,

husked and silks removed,

each about 3 inches long

◆

Combine all the ingredients except the corn in a large, stainless-steel or other nonreactive saucepan and bring to a boil over high heat. Add the corn, reduce the heat to medium, and simmer for 1 minute. Remove from the heat and let cool to room temperature. Using a slotted spoon, transfer the corn to dry, sterilized jars with lids. Add the vinegar mixture to within ½ inch of the rims. Cover with the lids and refrigerate.

The pickles will be ready to eat in 12 hours. They will keep for up to several weeks.

Makes about 2½ pints

Brined Grape Leaves

*E*ACH SUMMER WHEN PREPARING GRAPE LEAVES FOR BRINING, I FEEL AS IF I AM PRESERVING A LITTLE OF THE ROMANCE THAT VINEYARDS HAVE ALWAYS HELD FOR ME. FOLDING THE BRIGHT GREEN LEAVES OF SUMMER VINES AND TUCKING THEM TIGHTLY INTO JARS, I MENTALLY CAPTURE THE AWESTRUCK FEELING I HAD WHEN I FIRST SAW THE SWEEP OF THE VINEYARDS THAT STRETCH ALONG THE RHINE RIVER VALLEY. THE VINES SEEMED TO SWIRL AND WEAVE AND CLIMB WITH THE CONTOUR OF THE LAND, THE VISTA BROKEN ONLY BY THE TALL CRUMBLING TOWERS OF CENTURIES-OLD CASTLES.

LATER IN THE YEAR, USING THE LEAVES TO WRAP TROUT FOR GRILLING OR TO FILL WITH A SAVORY STUFFING, THE ROMANCE OF THE VINEYARD RETURNS. THE SLIPPERY FRESH FISH ENCLOSED IN LEAVES AND THEN GRILLED OVER A HOT FIRE WILL ABSORB A HINT OF THE GRAPEVINE TASTE WHILE GIVING UP ITS SKIN TO THE LEAF, LEAVING ONLY SUCCULENT WHITE FLESH FOR THE GREEDY EATER.

◆

4 quarts water

25 to 30 grape leaves, stemmed

1/2 cup salt

◆

Pour 3 quarts of the water into a large saucepan and bring to a boil over high heat. Add half of the grape leaves and boil just long enough to blanch them and make them supple, about 1 minute. Using a slotted utensil or tongs, lift out the leaves, draining well, and spread them flat in a single layer on cloth or paper towels to dry. Repeat with the remaining leaves.

To make the brine, combine the salt and the remaining 1 quart water in a stainless-steel or other nonreactive saucepan and bring to a boil over high heat, stirring to dissolve the salt. Continue to boil and stir for 2 or 3 minutes. Remove from the heat and let cool completely.

While the brine is cooling, fold each grape leaf envelope style and tuck into clean, dry jars with sealable lids, packing them tightly as you go. Pour the cooled brine over the leaves, filling the jars to within 1/2 inch of the jar rims. Using a damp cloth, wipe the rims clean. Cover with the lids and process for 15 minutes in a hot-water bath (see instructions for processing cold-pack foods on page 21).

Remove the jars and let them cool for 12 hours or overnight. Check the lids for a complete seal.

Store the sealed jars in a cool, dark place. The leaves will keep for up to 1 year. Once opened, keep them refrigerated. Store any jar lacking a good seal in the refrigerator for up to 10 days.

To use the grape leaves, first soak them in cold water to cover for about 10 minutes to remove the excess saltiness. Grape leaves are edible and may be used as you would a cabbage leaf for wrapping.

Makes about 2 pints

Nectarine Mustard

Curt Clingman, longtime chef at Oliveto, a wonderful restaurant in Oakland, California, shared this recipe with me. It makes a tangy, rich coating for roast lamb or pork.

◆

2 cups diced, peeled nectarines
(about 3 pounds)

1 cup dry mustard

2$\frac{1}{2}$ cups water

4$\frac{1}{2}$ tablespoons
grated orange zest

1$\frac{1}{2}$ cups Champagne vinegar
or cider vinegar

1 tablespoon salt

Juice of $\frac{1}{2}$ lemon

◆

In a frying pan over medium heat, cook the nectarines, stirring constantly, for 3 or 4 minutes. Reduce the heat and simmer until the nectarines soften and start to release their juices, about 5 minutes longer.

Add the mustard, water, orange zest, vinegar, and salt to the pan and simmer over low heat until quite thick, about 1½ hours. Stir occasionally during the first hour, and then stir frequently during the last 30 minutes to prevent burning the thickening mustard. When done, it will have the consistency of thick yogurt.

Remove from the heat and stir in the lemon juice. Let cool, then spoon into dry, sterilized jars with lids. Cover tightly and store in the refrigerator. The mustard will keep for up to 3 months.

Makes about 3 half-pints

Yellow Tomato Ketchup

THIS SPICY TOMATO KETCHUP CAN BE SERVED IN MUCH THE SAME WAY AS APPLESAUCE—CHILLED OR AT ROOM TEMPERATURE AS AN ACCOMPANIMENT TO VEGETABLES, SUCH AS CRISPY POTATO PANCAKES, OR WITH OMELETS, FRITTATAS, SOUFFLÉS, PORK CHOPS, SAUSAGES, FISH, OR CHICKEN. ITS THICK, FAINTLY CHUNKY TEXTURE HAS APPLESAUCE'S FAMILIAR HINTS OF CLOVE, CINNAMON, AND LEMON, PLUS THE EXOTIC OVERTONES OF CORIANDER, GINGER, GARLIC, AND SWEET PEPPERS.

◆

10 large, very ripe yellow tomatoes
(about 5 pounds)

2 large yellow sweet peppers,
seeded, deribbed, and coarsely
chopped (about 1 1/2 pounds)

2 onions (about 3/4 pound)

10 cloves garlic

1 cup white wine vinegar

Juice and grated zest of 1/4 lemon

3/4 cup granulated sugar

1 1/2 teaspoons salt

2 teaspoons mustard seeds

1 tablespoon black peppercorns

1 tablespoon coriander seeds

1 teaspoon whole cloves

1 cinnamon stick,
about 1 inch long

1-inch-piece fresh ginger,
cut into 3 or 4 pieces

◆

Bring a large saucepan filled with water to a boil. Immerse the tomatoes in the boiling water for 30 seconds. Lift out the tomatoes with a slotted utensil and, when cool enough to handle, peel off the skins. Cut in half crosswise and squeeze gently to remove the seeds, using your fingertip to dislodge any that do not fall out easily.

Put the tomatoes, sweet peppers, onions, garlic, 1/2 cup of the vinegar, and the lemon zest and juice in a stainless-steel or other nonreactive saucepan large enough to hold all the ingredients eventually. Cook over medium heat, stirring frequently, until the vegetables are soft and cooked through, 15 to 20 minutes.

Transfer the vegetable mixture to a blender or to a food processor fitted with the steel blade. Process until coarsely puréed but not liquefied. Return the purée to the pan, and add the sugar, salt, and the remaining 1/2 cup vinegar.

Cut out an 8-inch square of cheesecloth. Place in the center the mustard seeds, peppercorns, coriander seeds, cloves, cinnamon stick, and ginger. Gather up the corners and tie them with kitchen string to make a spice bag. Add to the pan holding the purée.

Bring the vegetable mixture to a simmer over low heat and continue to simmer, stirring occasionally, until it thickens, about 1 hour. Watch carefully so it does not burn. The finished ketchup will be slightly thinner than most commercial ketchups.

Ladle the hot ketchup into clean, dry jars with sealable lids, filling the jars to within 1/2-inch of the rims. Using a damp cloth, wipe the rims clean. Cover with the lids and process for 30 minutes in a hot-water bath (see instructions for processing hot-pack foods on page 21).

Remove the jars and let them cool 12 hours or overnight. Check the lids for a complete seal. Store the sealed jars in a cool, dark place. The ketchup will keep for up to 1 year. Once opened, keep refrigerated. Store any jar lacking a good seal in the refrigerator for up to 10 days.

Makes about 2 quarts

Green or Purple Basil Vinegars

*S*OME TIME AGO I STOOD IN FRONT OF AN ARRAY OF EXQUISITE, JEWEL-TONED VINEGARS AT THE FAMED FAUCHON IN PARIS. SMALL, ELEGANT, AND EXPENSIVE BOTTLES OF VINAIGRE DE CASSIS, DE FRAISE, DE MYRTILLE, DE CERISE TOOK UP AN ENTIRE SHELF. I BOUGHT A BOTTLE OF DEEP PURPLE VINAIGRE DE CASSIS AND CAREFULLY PACKED IT IN MY CARRY-ON BAG. I USED IT ONLY ON SPECIAL OCCASIONS, AND THEN AS SPARINGLY AS POSSIBLE, BECAUSE I WANTED IT TO LAST FOREVER.

SINCE THEN, I HAVE DISCOVERED THAT HERB- AND FRUIT-INFUSED VINEGARS ARE QUITE SIMPLE TO MAKE. THE FLAVOR OF BASIL VINEGAR—OR ANY OTHER INFUSED VINEGAR—WILL VARY DEPENDING UPON THE STRENGTH AND VARIETY OF THE VINEGAR USED, AS WELL AS THE AMOUNT AND THE VARIETY OF FLAVORING. THE PURPLE BASIL PRODUCES A MAGNIFICENT DEEP BURGUNDY VINEGAR, A VISUAL TREAT, WITH A FINE, SLIGHTLY HOT BASIL TASTE. GREEN BASIL, ON THE OTHER HAND, COLORS THE VINEGAR TO A FAINT GREEN, AND THE RESULTING TASTE IS PURE BASIL, WITHOUT THE HINT OF HEAT FOUND IN THE PURPLE VARIETY.

◆

*1 cup loosely packed green
or purple basil sprigs
3½ cups distilled white wine vinegar*

◆

Gently crush the basil between your fingertips, just enough to begin releasing the volatile oils. Put the basil into a dry, sterilized jar with a lid. Pour in the vinegar and cover with the lid. Place the jar in a sunny location, indoors or outside, and let stand about 10 days, or until the vinegar has become infused with the flavor of the basil to your satisfaction.

Strain the vinegar through a sieve lined with several layers of cheesecloth; discard the basil. Decant into dry, sterilized bottles. Seal with corks and store the bottles in a cool, dark place. The vinegar will keep for up to 1 year.

Makes about 1½ pints

Lavender Syrup

*L*AVENDER IS GENERALLY THOUGHT OF IN A FLORAL RATHER THAN A CULINARY SENSE, BUT IT HAS A LONG HISTORY OF BEING USED TO MAKE HOT, TEALIKE INFUSIONS AND TO FLAVOR SUCH SWEETS AND BAKED GOODS AS ICE CREAMS, CUSTARDS, BREADS, AND COOKIES. THIS SYRUP IS DELICATELY SCENTED, SWEET, AND LIGHT, WITH ONLY THE FAINTEST TASTE OF THE FLOWER'S HEAVENLY PERFUME. IT GIVES EXOTIC FLAIR TO FRUIT SALADS, AND A DROP OR TWO IN A GLASS OF CHAMPAGNE MAKES AN ELEGANT APERITIF.

◆

4 cups water
2 cups granulated sugar
1/2 cup pesticide-free fresh lavender flowers, or 2 tablespoons dried lavender flowers

◆

Combine the water and sugar in a stainless-steel or other nonreactive saucepan and bring to a boil over high heat, stirring. Reduce the heat to medium and simmer, continuing to stir, until the sugar dissolves and a thin syrup forms, about 10 minutes. Remove from the heat, add the lavender blossoms, cover, and let stand overnight in a cool place.

The next day, strain the syrup through a sieve lined with several layers of cheesecloth; discard the blossoms. Decant into dry, sterilized bottles. Seal with corks and store the bottles in a cool, dark place. The syrup will keep for 3 months or more.

Makes about 2 pints

Dried Tomatoes

DRYING TOMATOES INTENSIFIES THEIR FLAVOR, BUT A FLAVORLESS TOMATO CANNOT BE TRANSFORMED INTO SOMETHING THAT TASTES GOOD. IF YOU START WITH SWEET, GARDEN-RIPENED SUMMER TOMATOES, YOUR DRIED TOMATOES WILL REFLECT THEIR CHARACTER. CONVERSELY, A MEDIOCRE FRESH TOMATO WILL MAKE AN EQUALLY INSIPID DRIED ONE.

VIRTUALLY ANY TOMATO VARIETY CAN BE SUCCESSFULLY DRIED, AND SOME OF THE MOST SHARPLY SWEET OF ALL ARE THE SMALL CHERRY TYPES. TWO VARIETIES, SWEET 100'S AND THE UNUSUAL GREEN GRAPE, MAKE EXCEPTIONALLY DELICIOUS DRIED TOMATOES, AND DRY MORE QUICKLY THAN THE LARGER ROMA OR OTHER PASTE TYPES TRADITIONALLY USED FOR DRYING.

ONCE DRIED, THE TOMATOES CAN BE PACKED INTO GLASS JARS AND COVERED WITH OLIVE OIL, OR THEY CAN BE STORED DRY IN JARS OR PAPER BAGS. IF KEPT DRY, BEFORE USING COVER WITH A LITTLE BOILING WATER AND LET STAND TO SOFTEN A BIT, THEN DRAIN AND USE IN SALADS, PIZZA TOPPINGS, BREADS, OR SAUCES.

◆

5 to 6 pounds fully ripe, garden-ripened tomatoes of any color and variety

◆

If you are using cherry or medium-size tomatoes, cut them in half lengthwise. If you are using large beefsteak varieties, slice them very thinly crosswise. Arrange the prepared tomatoes in a single layer on a non-metal screen, placing the halved tomatoes cut side down.

Put the screen in full sun with good air circulation. Partial sun will work, but it will take longer for the tomatoes to dry. Bring the tomatoes indoors each night so they will not absorb evening or morning moisture. The tomatoes are ready when the color has darkened and they have no evident juice or moist pulp but are still supple. This will take about 3 days in full, hot sun and 5 to 6 days in partial sun.

At this stage, the tomatoes may be stored in loosely folded paper bags and kept in a cool, dry place for several weeks. After that, they can be strung and hung as you would a garlic or chili braid, or stored loosely packed in dry, sterilized jars with tight-fitting lids, where they will keep for up to 1 year. Hang or store away from direct sunlight. Or the tomatoes can be packed into dry, sterilized jars, covered with olive oil, tightly covered, and stored in a cool, dark place. They will keep for up to 6 months.

Makes about ¾ pound

AUTUMN

✦

POMEGRANATE JELLY

POMEGRANATE VINEGAR

PICKLED CRAB APPLES

PEARS PICKLED IN MERLOT

FIGS PICKLED IN BALSAMIC VINEGAR

AND HERBES DE PROVENCE

FOLIE OF FALL FRUITS

QUINCE SLICES IN VANILLA SYRUP

ZANTE GRAPES IN ARMAGNAC

SALSA ALL'AGRESTO

ITALIAN WINE CONSERVE

PICKLED MUSHROOMS

CONFIT OF ROASTED LEEKS

GOAT CHEESE IN OLIVE OIL AND HERBS

CRACKED GREEN OLIVES

WITH FENNEL AND BAY LEAVES

PROVENÇAL HOT CHILI OIL

✦

In the Autumn . . .

Fall, like summer, produces a massive flush of fruits and vegetables ripening one on top of the other, overlapping and overwhelming. At the same time, faintly warm days signal the end of the harvest season and the beginning of winter's dormancy. Previous generations worked hardest in fall, preserving as many fruits and vegetables as they possibly could, knowing that winter was coming soon and there must be ample food in storage to feed the family until spring.   ♦   From fall's vast selection we have the luxury of choosing fruits and vegetables that seem especially precious, especially wondrous to have not just in winter, but also in spring and summer. Even with today's long-distance shipping and cold storage, there are still some fruits and vegetables that are available for only a few weeks during the fall, and those are the ones that attract me the most.   ♦   Pomegranates, the love apples of Persephone, hang from the tree branches even when the leaves have been shriveled by frost, and few tastes compare to that of deep garnet pomegranate jelly spread across a thick slice of homemade bread still warm from the oven. Tiny Zante grapes, each barely as large as the tip of one's little finger, make a brief appearance in the fall market, often under the name Champagne grapes. Their delicate clusters and sweet taste warrant the extravagance of preserving a few in Armagnac. ◆ Green olives, of course, can be had for only a brief time before the chill nights begin to brush them first with purple, then with inky black. Even though the heavily laden trees cause me to want to make lots of different styles of preserved olives, it seems most important to put up one or two jars of fall's cracked green olives, since the window of opportunity is so fleeting. ◆ Crab apples, wild mushrooms, and quinces are other exceptional fall rewards. I like to preserve their tastes to remind me later of autumn's changing slant of light, its orange and purple sunsets, and the smell of cold on the morning air that intimates winter is coming—but not yet here.

Pomegranate Jelly

POMEGRANATES WERE PART OF MY CHILDHOOD, WITH ALMOST EVERY HOUSE IN THE NEIGHBORHOOD BOASTING A TREE. COME FALL, WHEN THE FRUITS RIPENED, WE ALTERNATED BETWEEN FLINGING THEM FROM OUR FORTS, WHERE THEY WERE STACKED UP LIKE CANNONBALLS, AND BLISSFULLY SITTING ON THE CURB AND EATING THEM. PICKING THE SEEDS OUT ONE BY ONE, WE TALKED AND PLAYED UNTIL WE WERE CALLED HOME AT SUNSET, OUR HANDS AND CLOTHES NOW SPECKLED CRIMSON WITH JUICE.

NOT UNTIL I MOVED TO NORTHERN CALIFORNIA AS AN ADULT DID I DISCOVER POMEGRANATE JELLY, WHICH HAS BECOME MY FAVORITE OF ALL JELLIES. IT IS TART AND SWEET AT THE SAME TIME, AND NOT THE LEAST BIT CLOYING.

◆

About 20 pomegranates
1 package powdered pectin
(1³/₄ ounces)
5 cups granulated sugar

◆

Cut the pomegranates in half. Put each half in an orange juice extractor and squeeze. Rinse a jelly bag with water, wring it out well, and hang the bag over a bowl. Immediately strain the juice through it. You will need 3½ cups juice.

Pour the strained juice into a stainless-steel or other nonreactive saucepan, add the pectin, and stir for several minutes to dissolve the pectin thoroughly. Place the pan over medium heat and bring the mixture to a boil, stirring constantly. Add the sugar and continue to stir constantly until the mixture is at a bubbling, rolling boil. Boil for 2 minutes, then begin to test for the jell point (see instructions on page 22). Alternatively, insert a candy thermometer in the mixture. When it reads 220 degrees F, the jelly is ready.

Remove from the heat. Skim off and discard any surface foam. Ladle the hot jelly into hot, dry sterilized jars, filling to within a ½ inch of the rims. Seal with a ⅛-inch-thick layer of melted paraffin (see directions for working with paraffin on page 22). Allow that layer to harden, then add a second layer of the same thickness. Using a damp cloth, wipe the rims clean. Cover with lids, aluminum foil, or with waxed paper or cotton cloth tightly fastened with twine or a rubber band.

Store in a cool, dark place. The jelly will keep for up to 1 year.

Makes 3 pints

Pomegranate Vinegar

*T*HE SHARP, TART TANG OF POMEGRAN-
ATE VINEGAR IS IDEAL FOR MEAT MARINADES OR
FOR DRESSINGS FOR FRUIT SALADS.

◆

1 cup pomegranate seeds
2 cups white wine vinegar

◆

Put the pomegranate seeds into a dry, sterilized jar with a lid. Pour in the vinegar and cover with the lid. Place the jar in a sunny location, indoors or outside, and let stand for 8 to 10 days, or until the vinegar has become infused with the flavor of pomegranate to your satisfaction.

Strain the vinegar through a sieve lined with several layers of cheesecloth; discard the seeds. Decant into dry, sterilized bottles. Seal with corks and store the bottles in a cool, dark place. The vinegar will keep for up to 6 months.

Makes 1 pint

Pickled Crab Apples

THESE SMALL, MOUTH-PUCKERING
APPLES HAVE BEEN OUT OF FASHION FOR MANY
YEARS, SO THEY ARE SOMETIMES DIFFICULT TO
FIND. IN SOME APPLE ORCHARDS, CRAB APPLES
ARE INTERPLANTED AMONG THE APPLES TREES TO
ACT AS POLLINATORS, BUT THEIR FRUITS AREN'T
SOLD. WHEN VISITING A ROADSIDE FRUIT STAND
OR FARMER'S MARKET, ASK THE GROWERS IF THEY
HAVE CRAB APPLES AS WELL AS APPLES. THE
TART PICKLED CRAB APPLES ARE SUCH A FINE
ACCOMPANIMENT TO ROAST PORK AND OTHER RICH
FOODS THAT IT IS WORTHWHILE TO SEEK OUT A
SOURCE.

◆

2 cups cider vinegar
2 cups granulated sugar
4 whole cloves
1 cinnamon stick,
about 2 inches long
3 pounds firm crab apples,
with stems intact if possible

◆

Combine the vinegar, sugar, cloves, and cinnamon in a stainless-steel or other nonreactive pan large enough to hold all the crab apples eventually. Bring to a boil over high heat and stir until the sugar dissolves, 2 or 3 minutes. Reduce the heat to medium, add the fruit, and cook until barely done, 5 or 6 minutes.

Using a slotted utensil, pack the crab apples into clean, dry jars with sealable lids. Ladle in the hot syrup to within ½ inch of the rims. Using a damp cloth, wipe the rims clean. Cover with the lids and process for 40 minutes in a hot-water bath (see instructions for processing hot-pack foods on page 21).

Remove the jars and let them cool for 12 hours or overnight. Check the jars for a complete seal.

Store the sealed jars in a cool, dark place. The crab apples will keep for up to 1 year. Once opened, keep them refrigerated. Store any jar lacking a good seal in the refrigerator for up to 10 days.

Makes 2 quarts

Pears Pickled in Merlot

OF THE MANY PRESERVES MADE BY MY GRANDMOTHER, ONE OF THE FEW MADE ALSO BY MY MOTHER WAS PICKLED PEACHES. EVERY SUMMER MOTHER MADE TWO OR THREE LARGE JARS, AND WE GENERALLY ATE THEM DURING THE CHRISTMAS HOLIDAYS. WHEN I WAS FIRST MARRIED, I, TOO, PUT UP PICKLED PEACHES. THESE WINE-INFUSED PICKLED PEARS ARE A MORE ELEGANT PREPARATION, AND I THINK MORE VERSATILE.

THE PEARS, WITH THEIR HINT OF WINE, CINNAMON, AND ROSEMARY, GO EQUALLY WELL WITH ROASTED MEATS OR COOKED BEANS SUCH AS BLACK-EYED PEAS, OR THEY CAN BE SERVED FOR DESSERT, ALONE OR WITH ICE CREAM, CAKE, OR COOKIES.

◆

10 firm pears
such as Red Bartlett or Bosc
(about 3½ pounds)
1 fifth Merlot
3 cups red wine vinegar
6 cups granulated sugar
1 tablespoon chopped
fresh rosemary
3 cinnamon sticks,
each about 4 inches long

◆

Peel the pears, leaving the stems intact. Set aside.

Combine the wine, vinegar, sugar, rosemary, and cinnamon in a stainless-steel or other nonreactive pan large enough to hold all the whole pears eventually. Bring to a boil over high heat. Boil, stirring often, until a thin syrup forms, about 5 minutes. Using a slotted utensil, slip the pears into the boiling syrup. Reduce the heat to medium and gently boil the pears, turning them in the syrup, until just barely cooked, 8 to 10 minutes. Be careful not to overcook them to the point where they become mushy.

Using a slotted utensil, transfer the pears to clean, dry jars with sealable lids. To pack the pears, make a layer of pears, standing them upright, then add a second layer of pears, inverting them, to maximize the space. Ladle in the hot syrup, including the cinnamon sticks, to cover the pears completely and to fill the jars to within ½ inch of the rims. Using a damp cloth, wipe the rims clean. Cover with the lids and process for 1 hour in a hot-water bath (see instructions for processing hot-pack foods on page 21).

Remove the jars and let them cool for 12 hours or overnight. Check for complete seals.

Store the sealed jars in a cool, dark place. The pears will keep for up to 1 year. Once opened, keep refrigerated. Store any jar lacking a complete seal in the refrigerator for up to 10 days.

Makes 3 pints

Figs Pickled in Balsamic Vinegar and Herbes de Provence

A FEW YEARS AGO I WAS IN THE BOULANGERIE OF A BACK-COUNTRY VILLAGE IN HAUTE-PROVENCE. ON DISPLAY IN ADDITION TO LOAVES OF BREAD, CROISSANTS, PAIN AU CHOCOLAT, AND THE USUAL BAKERY ASSORTMENT OF WRAPPED CANDIES AND HARD COOKIES, THERE STOOD A SHORT ROW OF GLASS JARS BANDED WITH HAND-PRINTED LABELS AND TOPPED WITH TWINE-TIED CAPS OF YELLOW-AND-RED PROVENÇAL CLOTH. A WHITE CARD SIGNALED FAIT Á LA MAISON—"HOMEMADE." ON CLOSER INSPECTION I SAW THE JARS CONTAINED FIGUES AUX HERBES DE PROVENCE. NATURALLY I BOUGHT ONE.

THE INTENSE SUGAR TYPICAL OF FALL FIGS WAS TEMPERED BY A SWEET-SOUR SYRUP, AND THROUGHOUT WAS THE SURPRISING PEPPERY, UNDERBRUSH TASTE OF THE WOODY THYME AND JUNIPER OF THE REGION'S BRUSH. EVEN THOUGH I INTENDED TO, I NEVER RETURNED TO THE BOULANGERIE TO TELL THE OWNERS HOW WON-DERFUL THE PICKLED FIGS WERE AND TO FIND OUT EXACTLY HOW THEY WERE MADE. ON RETURNING TO CALIFORNIA I PUT UP MY OWN VERSION, BASED ON MY MEMORY OF THE TASTE.

◆

1¹/₂ cups granulated sugar

3 cups water

6 allspice berries

4 tablespoons

chopped fresh thyme leaves

2 teaspoons

chopped fresh rosemary leaves

4 juniper berries

4 fresh or dried bay leaves

1 piece dried orange peel,

about 2 inches long,

plus 3 additional pieces,

each about 1 inch long

3¹/₂ pounds firm, ripe figs such as

Mission or Adriatic

³/₄ cup balsamic vinegar

3 fresh thyme sprigs,

each 2 inches long

3 fresh rosemary sprigs,

each 1 inch long

◆

Combine the sugar and water in a stainless-steel or other nonreactive saucepan large enough to hold the figs eventually. Bring to a boil over high heat, stirring to dissolve the sugar, then reduce the heat to medium and simmer until a light syrup forms, 5 to 7 minutes.

Meanwhile, cut out an 8-inch square of cheesecloth. Place in the center the allspice berries, chopped thyme and rosemary, juniper berries, bay leaves, and the 2-inch-piece orange peel. Gather up the corners and tie them with kitchen string to make a spice bag. Add the spice bag to the syrup, reduce the heat to low, and simmer for 20 minutes.

Add the figs to the simmering syrup. Continue to cook over low heat for 15 minutes, turning the figs gently from time to time. Remove the spice bag and discard. Using a slotted utensil, firmly pack the figs into 3 clean, dry half-pint jars with sealable lids. Divide the vinegar equally among the jars, then cover the fruit with the hot syrup to within ½ inch of the rims. Tuck a sprig each of thyme and rosemary, a bay leaf, and a 1-inch-piece orange peel into each jar. Using a damp cloth, wipe the rims clean. Cover with the lids and process for 20 minutes in a hot-water bath (see instructions for processing hot-pack foods on page 21).

Remove the jars and let them cool 12 hours or overnight. Check for a complete seal.

Store the sealed jars in a cool, dark place. The figs will keep for up to 1 year. Once opened, keep refrigerated. Store any jars lacking a good seal in the refrigerator for up to 1 week.

Makes 3 half-pints

Folie of Fall Fruits

*T*HIS IS A FALL VERSION OF THE FRENCH VIEUX GARÇON, OR BACHELOR'S BRAN-
DIED FRUIT. FOR THAT CLASSIC PREPARATION, LAYERS OF FRUIT, STARTING IN JUNE WITH
CHERRIES, ARE PUT INTO A CROCK, MASKED WITH SUGAR, AND THEN COVERED WITH BRANDY
OR OTHER SPIRITS. AS OTHER FRUITS RIPEN THROUGHOUT THE SUMMER, THEY ARE ADDED TO
THE CROCK, ALONG WITH MORE SUGAR AND BRANDY, AND SO ON THROUGHOUT THE FALL.
THEN, THROUGHOUT THE WINTER, THE BRANDIED FRUITS ARE EATEN. I HAVE NEVER LEARNED
WHETHER THE NAME COMES FROM THE IDEA THAT VIEUX GARÇON IS EASY ENOUGH FOR A
BACHELOR TO MAKE, OR BECAUSE IT CONTAINS ENOUGH BRANDY FOR A LONELY BACHELOR TO
DROWN HIS SORROWS.

THIS VERSION USES GRAPES, APPLES, AND PEARS OF DIFFERENT COLORS AND VARIET-
IES. PERSIMMONS AND BERRIES COULD ALSO BE USED.

◆

4 firm, slightly underripe pears,
such as Bosc or Red Bartlett
2 firm apples,
such as Granny Smith or Gala
1 small bunch purple grapes
(about 1/3 pound)
1 small bunch green or rose grapes
(about 1/3 pound)
3 cups brandy
3 cups granulated sugar

◆

Peel and core the pears and apples, then cut them lengthwise into slices 1 inch thick. Stem the grapes, discarding any grapes that are bruised or damaged.

Combine the brandy and the sugar in a stainless-steel or other nonreactive pan large enough to hold all the fruits eventually. Bring to a boil over high heat, then reduce the heat to low and simmer, stirring, until the sugar dissolves, 2 to 3 minutes. Add the sliced fruits and grapes and simmer another 2 to 3 minutes. The fruits will change color slightly and will offer resistance when pricked with the tines of a fork.

Using a slotted utensil, lightly pack the fruits into hot, dry, sterilized jars with lids. Pour in the hot syrup to cover the fruits completely. At first the fruits will float toward the top, but as they eventually absorb the sugar they will sink to the bottom. Cover with the lids.

Store in a cool, dark place for a least 4 weeks to allow the flavors to develop. Open the lids every few days for a moment to allow any fermenting gases to escape. The fruits will keep 4 months or more in a cool, dark place or they may be refrigerated.

Makes about 3 pints

Quince Slices in Vanilla Syrup

QUINCE IS AN EXCEPTIONAL FRUIT THAT WAS FAR MORE POPULAR AND AVAIL-ABLE IN THE PAST. BECAUSE OF THEIR HIGH-PECTIN CONTENT, QUINCES WERE FREQUENTLY COMBINED WITH LOW-PECTIN FRUITS AS WELL AS PREPARED ON THEIR OWN. ALTHOUGH INEDIBLE WHEN RAW, THEY TAKE ON A HONEYED SWEETNESS AKIN TO ASIAN PEARS WHEN COOKED IN A SYRUP, AS THEY ARE HERE.

THE FRUITS ALSO CHANGE THEIR COLOR WHEN COOKED, TURNING FROM PASTY WHITE TO A DEEP ROSE-AMBER. THESE VANILLA-INFUSED SLICES CAN BE EATEN AS A COMPOTE, WARM OR COLD. THEY MAY ALSO BE SERVED ON THEIR OWN AS A CONDIMENT TO ACCOMPANY ANY SAVORY DISH OR USED AS A PIE FILLING. I FIND THEM ESPECIALLY GOOD AT BREAKFAST, WHEN I LIKE TO SLIP A SPOONFUL OR TWO INTO WARM OATMEAL WITH A LITTLE CREAM.

❖

6 quinces (about 3 pounds)

4 cups granulated sugar

4 cups water

1 vanilla bean,
about 8 inches long

2 tablespoons fresh lemon juice

❖

Peel and core the quinces and carefully remove and discard the seeds. Cut the fruits lengthwise into slices ½ inch thick. Set aside.

Combine the sugar, water, vanilla bean, and lemon juice in a stain-less-steel or other non-reactive saucepan large enough to hold the quince eventually. Bring the mixture to a boil over medium-high heat and continue to boil, stirring often, until a light- to medium-thick syrup forms, about 10 minutes. Reduce the heat and add the quince slices. Poach the fruits until just barely tender when pierced with the tines of a fork, about 15 minutes. Cooking time will vary depending upon the maturity of the fruits.

Using a slotted utensil, tightly pack the quince slices into clean, dry jars with sealable lids. Ladle in the hot syrup to within ½ inch of the rims. Using a damp cloth, wipe the rims clean. Cover with the lids and process for 40 minutes in a hot-water bath (see instructions for processing hot-pack foods page 21).

Remove the jars and let them cool for at least 12 hours or overnight. Check the lids for a complete seal.

Store the sealed jars in a cool, dark place. The quince slices will keep for up to 1 year. Once opened, keep them refrigerated. Store any jar lacking a good seal in the refrigerator for up to 1 week.

Makes about 4 pints

Zante Grapes in Armagnac

ZANTE GRAPES, GROWN PRIMARILY FOR DRYING TO BE SOLD AS CURRANTS, ARE RARELY LARGER THAN A SMALL PEA AND OFTEN THE SIZE OF A PLUMP PEPPERCORN. BECAUSE OF THEIR MINUSCULE SIZE AND TIGHTLY BUNCHED GROWTH HABIT, SWEET, BERRY-FLAVORED ZANTES ARE BEST EATEN BY THE CLUSTER RATHER THAN ONE BY ONE, AND THEY CAN BE PRESERVED IN CLUSTERS AS WELL.

ONLY A RELATIVELY SMALL AMOUNT OF ZANTE GRAPES REACH THE FRESH MARKET, APPEARING FOR A FEW WEEKS IN FALL. THEY ARE FREQUENTLY PROMOTED AS CHAMPAGNE GRAPES, THE MARKETING IDEA BEING TO DROP A FEW GRAPES INTO A GLASS OF CHAMPAGNE WHERE THE TINY, PALE ROSE SPHERES SEEM LIKE BUBBLES.

CERTAINLY THESE ARMAGNAC-PRESERVED ZANTE GRAPES MAY BE ADDED TO CHAMPAGNE, BUT LIKE JUDY ROGERS, THE CHEF AT SAN FRANCISCO'S ZUNI CAFE WHO GAVE ME THIS RECIPE, I PREFER TO PARTNER THE PICKLED GRAPES WITH SAVORY, STRONG-FLAVORED DISHES SUCH AS ROAST DUCK OR PHEASANT, ADDING THEM TO THE SAUCE CREATED FROM THE PAN JUICES.

◆

1^1/$_2$ pounds Zante grape bunches

^{2}/$_3$ cup granulated sugar

1^1/$_2$ cups Armagnac

or other brandy

◆

Separate the bunches into clusters about 1 inch across, removing and discarding any damaged grapes. Put the clusters into a dry, sterilized widemouthed jar with a lid. Sprinkle the sugar over the grape clusters and pour in the Armagnac. Cover with the lid.

Place in a cool, dark place or in the refrigerator. Every day turn and jostle the jar until the sugar dissolves completely. This will take about 10 days.

The grapes will be ready in about 2 weeks, but the flavor will mellow over time. Store in a cool, dark place. The grapes will keep for up to 1 year.

Makes about 1½ pints

Salsa all'Agresto

Marco Fiorini, chef at San Francisco's elegant Blue Fox restaurant, told me of this traditional recipe. His family is from the Valtellina, a rugged, steeply narrow alpine valley northeast of Milan that climbs steadily from the far reaches of Lake Como to the Swiss border. Marco told me this sauce has been made in the region since the Middle Ages.

Used in place of vinegar, the juice of unripened grapes is the source of the sauce's tart, unusual taste, with bread, herbs, and almonds composing the balance. The sauce has a particular affinity for veal and trout, which is unsurprising when one considers that the Valtellina has both numerous dairies and many streams in the surrounding mountains.

◆

*1 large bunch unripened table
or wine grapes such as
Concord, Thompson seedless,
or Cabernet Sauvignon
(about 1¹/₂ pounds)
¹/₂ cup fine fresh bread crumbs
1 teaspoon granulated sugar
2 tablespoons
chopped fresh parsley
¹/₂ teaspoon salt
¹/₂ teaspoon
freshly ground black pepper
2 garlic cloves
¹/₂ cup unsalted almonds
¹/₄ cup chicken stock,
if serving sauce heated*

◆

Discard any grapes that are bruised or damaged. Crush the grapes, using a mortar and pestle, in a bowl with the back of a wooden spoon, or in a food mill. Strain the juice through a fine mesh sieve and discard the skins, seeds, and stems. You should have approximately 1 cup juice; set aside.

Combine the bread crumbs, sugar, parsley, salt, pepper, garlic, and almonds in a blender or a food processor fitted with the steel blade. Purée the mixture.

Slowly add the grape juice and process until a thick paste forms.

Spoon the paste into a dry, sterilized jar with a lid. Cover and refrigerate for up to 1 week.

The sauce may be used chilled, at room temperature, or heated. To use the sauce warm, place the chicken stock in a saucepan and stir in the sauce. Heat gently; do not let the mixture boil or the sauce will separate.

Makes about ¾ pint

Italian Wine Conserve

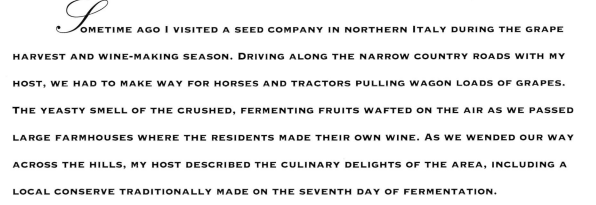

Sometime ago I visited a seed company in northern Italy during the grape harvest and wine-making season. Driving along the narrow country roads with my host, we had to make way for horses and tractors pulling wagon loads of grapes. The yeasty smell of the crushed, fermenting fruits wafted on the air as we passed large farmhouses where the residents made their own wine. As we wended our way across the hills, my host described the culinary delights of the area, including a local conserve traditionally made on the seventh day of fermentation.

As I understood it, the froth of the fermenting wine is skimmed, and the skimmings are then combined with sugar and cooked into a thick jam to which small pieces of dried apricots, pears, and walnuts are added. Unfortunately, I never got to try it, but I devised this recipe based on how I imagined it would taste.

✦

1 quince

1 bunch grapes,

preferably Concord, Zinfandel,

or another wine grape

(about 1 1/2 pounds)

1 cup fruity wine

such as Gamay Beaujolais

2 cups granulated sugar

1 lemon zest strip,

about 1 inch long

1/2 cup chopped dried apricots

3/4 cup chopped dried pears

1 cup chopped walnuts

✦

Peel and core the quince and carefully remove and discard the seeds. Grate the quince and set aside. Discard any grapes that are bruised or damaged. Crush the grapes, using a mortar with a pestle, in a bowl with the back of a wooden spoon, or in a food mill. Strain the juice through a fine-mesh sieve and discard the skins, seeds, and stems. You should have approximately 1 cup juice; set aside.

Combine the grape juice, wine, sugar, quince, and lemon zest in a stainless-steel or other nonreactive sauce-pan. Bring to a boil over medium-high heat, stirring to dissolve the sugar. Continue to boil, stirring constantly, until the mixture thickens, about 15 minutes. Stir in the apricots and pears and cook for another 15 minutes. Stir in the walnuts. Remove from the heat.

Ladle the conserve into clean, dry jars with sealable lids, filling the jars to within a 1/2 inch of the rims. Using a damp cloth, wipe the rims clean. Cover with the lids and process for 40 minutes in a hot-water bath (see instructions for processing hot-pack foods on page 21).

Remove the jars and let them cool for 12 hours or overnight. Check for complete seals.

Store the sealed jars in a cool, dark place. The conserve will keep for up to 1 year. Once opened, keep them refrigerated. Store any jar lacking a good seal in the refrigerator for up to 2 weeks.

Makes 1 1/2 pints

From left to right:
Italian Wine Conserve
Cracked Green Olives
with Fennel and Bay Leaves
Pomegranate Jelly
Pickled Mushrooms
Figs Pickled in Balsamic Vinegar
Confit of Roasted Leeks
Pomegranate Vinegar
Pickled Crab Apples

Pickled Mushrooms

*W*ITHOUT QUESTION, FALL IS MUSHROOM SEASON. LATE-SUMMER RAINS COMBINE WITH THE STILL-WARM DAYS OF FALL TO CREATE THE IDEAL CONDITIONS FOR THE FUNGI TO POP UP ON FOREST BEDS, ACROSS HILLSIDES, AND THROUGHOUT MEADOWS. ONE OF THE MOST SATISFYING ACTIVITIES OF THE SEASON IS COLLECTING WILD MUSHROOMS, A PLEASURE I FIRST DISCOVERED WHILE LIVING IN FRANCE. IT SO HAPPENED THAT IT WAS ONE OF THOSE RARE YEARS WHEN THE ELEMENTS CAME TOGETHER IN A PERFECT CONFIGURATION FOR ABUNDANT AND EXTENDED MUSHROOM GROWTH.

DAY AFTER DAY FOR ALMOST A MONTH, MY NEIGHBORS CAME BACK FROM THE SURROUNDING COUNTRYSIDE LADEN WITH BASKETS OF CÉPES, CHANTERELLES, AND SANGUINES—MORE THAN COULD POSSIBLY BE EATEN FRESH. I SPENT HOURS HELPING THEM SLICE THE MUSHROOMS FOR PICKLING OR FOR STRINGING THEM FOR DRYING. MONTHS LATER, ON A COLD DECEMBER NIGHT AS PART OF THE CHRISTMAS HORS D'OEUVRE OFFERING, WE ATE THE PICKLED MUSHROOMS WITH THE TASTE OF THE FALL FOREST STILL IN THEM.

◆

1/2 cup olive oil

1/2 cup balsamic vinegar

3/4 teaspoon salt

1/2 teaspoon black peppercorns

4 fresh thyme sprigs,

each 3 inches long

1/2 pound firm fresh mushrooms

such as cèpe, shiitake, or button,

cut into 1/2-inch-thick slices

◆

To make the pickling mixture, combine ¼ cup each of the olive oil and vinegar in a stainless-steel or other nonreactive saucepan. Add the salt, peppercorns, and thyme and bring to a boil over medium-high heat. Boil for 2 minutes, then add the sliced mushrooms and reduce the heat to very low. Cook for 2 minutes longer, turning the mushrooms constantly.

Ladle the mushroom mixture into a dry, sterilized jar with a lid. Add the remaining olive oil and vinegar and cover the jar loosely with aluminum foil or waxed paper. Let cool to room temperature.

Discard the foil or waxed paper and cover with the lid. Refrigerate at least 24 hours to allow the flavors to develop before using. The oil will solidify somewhat, but will liquefy again at room temperature. The mushrooms may be stored in the refrigerator for up to 3 months.

Makes about 1 pint

Confit of Roasted Leeks

*I*N LATE FALL, THE FIRST CROP OF
LEEKS, PLANTED FROM SEEDLINGS SET OUT IN
EARLY SUMMER, IS READY TO HARVEST. NOT YET
HUGE NOR TOUGHENED BY FREEZING TEMPERA-
TURES, THE EARLY LEEKS ARE TENDER AND
SWEET AND THEIR NATURAL SUGAR READILY
CARAMELIZES DURING SLOW ROASTING. THEY
EMERGE FROM THE OVEN A DELICATE SHADE OF
CREAMY GOLD, TASTING SO GOOD THAT YOUR
PREDILECTION WILL BE TO EAT THEM IMMEDI-
ATELY RATHER THAN PUT THEM INTO YOUR
GLASS PANTRY.

LEEK CONFIT, WARM OR COLD, MAKES A
FLAVORFUL SPREAD FOR SANDWICHES, IS A GOOD
PIZZA TOPPING, OR CAN BE USED TO ENRICH SOUPS
OR STEWS.

◆

4 pounds young leeks
Butter, for greasing pan
1/2 cup olive oil
2 teaspoons salt
2 teaspoons granulated sugar

◆

Preheat an oven to 350 degrees F.

Wash the leeks well to remove any gritty bits of sand and soil caught between the layers of leaves. Neatly trim off the fibrous roots and the uppermost dark green leaves and discard. Cut the leeks, both the white and green parts, into ¼-inch-thick slices.

Butter a shallow baking pan large enough to hold the sliced leeks in a layer 1 inch deep. Add the leeks, drizzle the olive oil on them, then sprinkle with salt and sugar.

Put the leeks in the preheated oven and roast, turning often, until they appear melted and are a creamy gold, 45 minutes to 1 hour.

Remove them from the oven and let cool to room temperature. Spoon the leeks into dry, sterilized jars with lids. Cover and store in the refrigerator. The leeks will keep for up to 2 weeks.

Makes about 2 pints

WHEN I WAS LIVING IN FRANCE, I MADE AND SOLD FRESH GOAT CHEESES. ONE OF MY FIRST CUSTOMERS WAS AN AUBERGE LOCATED NEXT TO AN OLD CHURCH IN A MEDIEVAL VILLAGE PRECARIOUSLY PERCHED ATOP A HILL. THE SETTING WAS FORMIDABLE, AS WAS THE COOK, WHO HAD A REPUTATION FOR BEING TEMPERAMENTAL, SO I ALWAYS MADE MY DELIVERIES WITH A LITTLE TREPIDATION. ONE DAY I FOUND THE COOK IN AN EXPANSIVE MOOD AND WAS INVITED IN. THE RED-TILED KITCHEN WAS FILLED WITH BASKETS OF FRUITS AND VEGETABLES FROM THE GARDEN; BUNCHES OF WILD HERBS FESTOONED THE OPEN FIREPLACE AND HAND-HEWN, DARK WOODEN WORK TABLES SAT SQUARELY IN THE CENTER. I WAS ENTRANCED.

THE COOK, WHOSE NAME I HAVE SINCE FORGOTTEN, TOOK ME OVER TO A SIDEBOARD AND SHOWED ME A LARGE GLASS JAR HALF FULL OF BITS AND CHUNKS OF GOAT CHEESE RESTING IN RICH GREEN OLIVE OIL FLAVORED WITH PEPPERCORNS AND HERBS. THE SUN, COMING THROUGH A PANED WINDOW, CAST THE EDGE OF THE JAR IN LIGHT, AND THE WHOLE ARRAY OF LIGHT AND RICH COLORS LOOKED LIKE AN ARTIST'S COMPOSITION. THE COOK EXPLAINED THAT HIS CUSTOMERS WERE PLEASED WITH MY FRESH CHEESE, SO TO PRESERVE ITS FRESHNESS AND PREVENT IT FROM DRYING OUT, HE ALWAYS PUT ANY LEFTOVER CHEESE INTO THE OLIVE OIL. THAT WAY, BETWEEN MY TWICE-WEEKLY DELIVERIES, HE WOULD ALWAYS HAVE "FRESH" CHEESE.

ONCE HOME, I TRIED IT WITH MY OWN CHEESE, AND ALTHOUGH IT WASN'T QUITE "FRESH" TO MY THINKING, I LOVED THE EXTRA TASTE AND RICHNESS IMPARTED BY THE SEASONED OIL. THEREAFTER, I KEPT A JAR OF CHEESE IN OLIVE OIL FOR THE BEAUTY OF IT, AS WELL AS FOR THE TASTE OF IT IN SALADS OR SIMPLY SPREAD ON A SLICE OF COUNTRY BREAD.

About 10 ounces firm,
fresh goat cheese,
whole or in pieces
12 black peppercorns
4 fresh or dried bay leaves
4 fresh thyme sprigs
3 fresh rosemary sprigs
2 cups olive oil

Put all of the ingredients
in a dry, sterilized jar
large enough for the
cheese to be covered
with the oil; the cheese
must not be tightly
packed. Let the cheese
mellow for a week before
sampling it.

Store in a cool, dark
place. The cheese will
keep for 1 or 2 months.

Makes 1 pint

Cracked Green Olives with Fennel and Bay Leaves

ALTHOUGH I ALWAYS THINK I AM GOING TO PUT UP VATS OF OLIVES, IN THE END I USUALLY PICK ONLY A FEW POUNDS OF GREEN OLIVES AND MAKE THIS TRADITIONAL RECIPE. IT CARRIES A SLIGHT TASTE OF BITTERNESS, WHICH I LIKE, AND THE OLIVES ARE BOLDLY FLAVORED BY THE SPICED BRINE.

THE ONLY DIFFICULTY THIS SIMPLE PREPARATION POSES IS THE NEED TO CHANGE THE WATER EVERY DAY FOR TWENTY-FIVE DAYS! THE WATER GRADUALLY LEACHES MOST OF THE BITTER GLUCOSIDE THAT MAKES FRESH-PICKED OLIVES INEDIBLE. AFTER THE GLUCOSIDE HAS DEPARTED, THE OLIVES ARE PACKED IN BRINE.

◆

*2 pounds unblemished
bright green olives
2 cups salt
2 cups water
3 fresh or dried bay leaves
2 flowering fennel tops; 3 fennel
stalks, each 2 inches long;
or 1/2 teaspoon fennel seeds
1 piece dried orange peel,
about 2 inches long
1 tablespoon coriander seeds*

◆

Working with 1 olive at a time, place on a firm work surface. With a wooden mallet or heavy knife handle, hit the olive sufficiently to crack open the skin. If you hit an olive so hard the skin breaks away, discard it. Place the cracked olives in a large ceramic or other nonreactive container and add water to cover. Then change the water each day. I keep the olives in a colander so I can remove them easily and set them aside while I fill the container with fresh water. As the olives soak in the water, you will see them begin to change color. The longer they soak, the darker they gradually become. In the tradition of Provence, the olives soak only 9 days, but at that stage the olives are still too bitter for my taste. I suggest soaking them for 25 days, but generally start tasting the olives after 2 weeks. When the olives are ready, drain and rinse them in cold water. Set aside.

To prepare the brine, combine all the remaining ingredients in a stainless-steel or other nonreactive saucepan and bring to a boil over high heat. Continue to boil for 5 minutes, stirring often, then remove from the heat and let the brine cool completely.

Put the drained, rinsed olives into a dry, sterilized jar and pour in enough brine, including the bay leaves and spices, to cover them. Cover the jar with a tight-fitting lid and store in the refrigerator. The olives will keep for 2 to 3 months.

Makes about 1½ pints

BOTTLES OF OLIVE OIL CONTAINING DRIED RED CHILIES, BLACK PEPPERCORNS, AND THE WILD HERBS OF THE REGION SIT ON THE TABLES OF EVERY PIZZERIA IN PROVENCE. WHEN A THIN, CRISP PIZZA IS SERVED DIRECTLY FROM THE WOOD-BURNING OVEN, THE FIRST THING TO DO IS TO SPRINKLE IT WITH SOME OF THE CHILI OIL.

THESE COLORFUL BOTTLES MAKE CHARMING GIFTS FOR PIZZA LOVERS, ESPECIALLY WHEN ACCOMPANIED WITH A PIZZA CUTTER, A BOUQUET OF DRIED HERBS, A SPECIAL CALABRIAN SAUSAGE, A BLOCK OF PARMIGIANO-REGGIANO, OR OTHER ACCOUTREMENTS ASSOCIATED WITH THE MAKING AND EATING OF PIZZA.

✦

1 tablespoon black peppercorns

3 fresh or dried bay leaves

5 small dried hot red chili

peppers, with seeds intact

3 fresh thyme sprigs,

each 3 to 4 inches long

2 cups olive oil

✦

In the order listed, put all of the ingredients into a dry, sterilized wine bottle. Seal with a cork and store in a cool, dark place for at least 2 or 3 weeks to allow time for the oil to become infused with the other flavors.

The oil will keep for several months. To make a sprinkler top, cut a ¼-inch-deep, V-shaped channel the length of the cork.

Makes 1 pint

WINTER

✦

Navel Orange Marmalade

Rose Hip Jelly

Candied Grapefruit Peel

Lemon Curd

Confit of Roasted Onions

Ancho Chili Sauce

Pickled Garlic Cloves

Pickled Whole Onions

Pink Pickled Shallots

Pickled Carrots

and Jalapeño Chilies

Whole Preserved Lemons

Spicy Lemon Oil

Vin d'Orange

Cayenne Walnuts

Salted Blanched Almonds

✦

In the Winter...

It seems fanciful to be thinking about making preserves of any kind when the fruit and nut trees stand bare and gaunt in the orchard, and the garden is empty of all but the most cold-hardy greens and frost-impervious roots. Yet winter, like other times of the year, has its seasonal specialties. ✦ Oranges, lemons, grapefruits—all of the citrus—come into season in winter. The lemons are the first of my citrus to ripen, and the early ones go into lemon curd for Christmas gift giving. Lemon oil and whole spiced lemons are so easy to make I can do them at the same time I prepare the lemon curd. ✦ The grapefruits on my trees—a Marsh variety—don't ripen early enough for me to use them to make candied peels for Christmas treats, so I buy Ruby or other grapefruits at the store. Best of all, my navel and blood orange trees start showing orangish gold balls by early November, and by Christmas Day I am drinking freshly squeezed orange juice and contemplating the making of vin d'orange. Shortly after the holidays, it is time to start putting up orange marmalade, and if it's too late to give for Christmas gifts, it is just right for winter and spring breakfasts. The marmalade, it seems, rarely lasts past May.

✦ Although citrus is certainly the most glamorous of winter's fare, the storage cellar holds some special ingredients, too. The onions, garlic, shallots, and chili peppers harvested in late summer and throughout the fall and the local almond and walnuts are ready for my attention. The nuts take readily to both sweet and savory coatings and the chilies can be turned into rich, dark sauces. Onions, garlic, and shallots are quick to pickle, whole or sliced, and I like using them both as condiments and as ingredients in other dishes. ✦ In fact, it is winter's preserves that I find the most enticing. The spicy scent of caramelizing orange peels, the sweet, heavy fragrance of grapefruit peels bubbling in clear sugar syrup, and the clean, sharp smell of fresh-picked lemons waft in and out of the kitchen, finally to be embodied in the marmalade, the vin d'orange, a spicy lemon oil, and other preserves. Winter's tastes are never out of season, even after the trees have resprouted leaves, the first asparagus is breaking through the soil, and the artichokes are beginning to bud.

Navel Orange Marmalade

FRETTING FOR YEARS BECAUSE I DIDN'T HAVE "REAL" SEVILLE BITTER ORANGES TO MAKE "REAL" MARMALADE, I FINALLY DECIDED I WAS BEING SILLY. AFTER ALL, I HAVE A DOZEN CALIFORNIA NAVEL ORANGE TREES AT MY HOUSE, ALL OF WHICH BEAR WONDERFUL FRUITS EVERY YEAR. CERTAINLY I COULD USE THEM TO MAKE A MARMALADE.

THE PERFECT OCCASION TO LAUNCH THE PROJECT WAS DURING THE VISIT OF A FRIEND FROM FRANCE. WE SPENT AN AROMATIC DAY EXPERIMENTING IN THE KITCHEN AND FINALLY ARRIVED AT THE FOLLOWING RECIPE.

THE METHODS AND THE RESULTS BOTH DEPART FROM CLASSIC ORANGE MARMALADE RECIPES IN SEVERAL WAYS BECAUSE THE NAVEL AND THE SEVILLE VARIETIES DIFFER CONSIDERABLY. THE SEEDLESS NAVEL IS SWEET AND HAS A THICK SKIN, WHILE THE SEVILLE ORANGE HAS MANY SEEDS, IS BITTER, AND HAS A THIN SKIN.

(CONTINUED ON PAGE 114)

IN ORANGE MARMALADE RECIPES USING SEVILLES, THE SEEDS ARE COLLECTED, TIED IN A CLOTH, AND COOKED ALONG WITH THE JUICE AND PULP. THIS STEP MUST OBVIOUSLY BE OMITTED WHEN USING NEAR-SEEDLESS NAVELS. THE WHITE, OR PITH, OF THE SEVILLE IS SCANT, WHILE THAT OF THE NAVEL IS THICK. IN THE CLASSIC RECIPES, ALL OF THE PITH IS INCLUDED, BUT IN THIS RECIPE ABOUT HALF IS TRIMMED AWAY AND DISCARDED, SINCE USING ALL OF IT WOULD IMPART A SPONGY TEXTURE TO THE PRESERVES.

FINALLY, IN THE INTEREST OF TIME, I HAVE DEVIATED FROM THE CLASSIC PREPARATION IN AN ACT THAT ALTERS THE AESTHETICS OF THE FINISHED MARMALADE. THE ORANGE OUTER SKIN, OR ZEST, IS TRADITIONALLY, AND QUITE BEAUTIFULLY, CUT BY HAND INTO THIN, THIN STRIPS THAT LOOK HIGHLY PRECISE. IN THIS RECIPE, ONLY ONE ORANGE SKIN IS CUT IN THIS FASHION AND THE OTHERS ARE CHOPPED.

THE APPEARANCE OF THE NAVEL MARMALADE IS CHUNKIER THAN THE CLASSIC, AND IT IS A STRIKING DEEP ORANGE, ALMOST AMBER. ITS TEXTURE IS SOLID AND DENSE, WHICH MEANS THAT IT CAN BE SUCCESSFULLY SEALED WITH PARAFFIN. AND THE TASTE? SWEETER THAN A BITTER ORANGE MARMALADE, BUT STILL WITH THAT EDGE OF BITTERNESS THAT DEFINES THESE DISTINCTIVE PRESERVES.

THE ORANGES HANG ON MY TREES LONGER THAN ON THOSE OF COMMERCIAL GROWERS, SO THE SUGAR CONTENT OF THE FRUIT IS HIGHER AND THE COLOR IS DEEPER THAN ORANGES FROM THE STORE. YOU MAY WANT TO INCREASE THE SUGAR IF THE FRUITS YOU ARE USING DO NOT SEEM SWEET ENOUGH.

12 navel oranges
(about 4 1/2 pounds)
4 lemons (about 1 1/2 pounds)
2 quarts water
5 pounds granulated sugar

Peel the oranges and lemons—zest only, no pith—as thinly as you can. Slice the peel from 1 orange into paper-thin strips about 1/16 inch wide. You will have about 1/4 cup. Put the remaining peels into a blender or a food processor fitted with the steel blade and chop.

Put the hand-sliced peel and the machine-chopped peel into a heavy-bottomed pan and add the water. Bring to a boil over high heat, then reduce the heat to medium and simmer until tender, about 20 minutes.

While the peels are simmering, prepare the pulp. Trim away and discard about half the pith from the oranges, then quarter them. Quarter the lemons. Cut both the lemon and the orange quarters into lengthwise slices 1/4 inch thick.

Add the orange and lemon slices to the simmering peels. Increase the heat to medium-high and cook, stirring often, for 15 minutes. Remove from the heat and let stand in a cool place for 24 hours.

The next day, return the pan to medium-high heat and add the sugar, stirring to dissolve it. Bring to a gentle boil and cook, stirring often, until the mixture becomes clear, 20 to 30 minutes, then begin to test for the jell point (see instructions on page 22). Alternatively, insert a candy thermometer in the mixture. When it reads 220 degrees F, the marmalade is ready.

Remove from the heat. Skim off and discard any surface foam. Ladle the marmalade into hot, dry, sterilized jars, filling to within 1/2 inch of the rims. Seal with a 1/8-inch-thick layer of melted paraffin (see directions for working with paraffin on page 22). Allow that layer to harden, then add a second layer of the same thickness. Using a damp cloth, wipe the rims clean. Cover with lids, aluminum foil, or with waxed paper or cotton cloth tightly fastened with twine or a rubber band.

Store in a cool, dark place. The marmalade will keep for up to 1 year.

Makes about 4 1/2 pints

Rose Hip Jelly

FROM THE GATHERING OF THE ROSE HIPS AND THE APPLES TO THE PLOP, PLOP OF THE JUICE DRIPPING THROUGH THE BAG, I AM FASCINATED BY THE PROCESS OF MAKING THIS JELLY BECAUSE IT IS SO BASIC AND CLOSE TO NATURE. FIRST I HARVEST THE LARGE, PLUMP RED-ORANGE ROSE HIPS FROM THE THORNY ROSA RUGOSA BUSHES THAT LINE MY ROAD. NEXT, I GO TO THE CELLAR AND BRING UP SOME OF THE TART GRANNY SMITH APPLES STORED THERE IN LATE OCTOBER. THE APPLES CONTAIN THE PECTIN NECESSARY FOR JELLING.

◆

8 to 10 tart green apples,
such as Granny Smith
1 pound rose hips (about 8 cups),
cut in half
2 quarts water
2 cups granulated sugar

◆

Coarsely chop the apples, including the cores and the seeds. Place in a saucepan with the rose hips and water and bring to a boil over high heat. Reduce the heat to medium-low and simmer until the apples are soft, 20 to 25 minutes. Remove from the heat.

Position a sieve over a container large enough to catch the drippings as they fall through the sieve. Pour the apple mixture into the sieve. With a pestle or the back of a wooden spoon, press against the pieces of apple and rose hip, pushing the resulting pulp through the holes of the sieve. Continue mashing until only skins and seeds remain in the sieve.

Rinse a jelly bag with water, wring it out well, and hang the bag over a large bowl. Transfer the pulpy sieved contents of the bowl to the bag. Leave it to drip. This is a slow process, and one that cannot be hurried!

After an hour or two, the juice will have dripped through. Put this juice in a nonreactive saucepan, add the sugar and, while stirring, bring it to a rolling boil over high heat. Reduce the heat slightly to a gentle boil and cook for approximately 20 minutes, then test for the jell point (see instructions on page 22). Alternatively, insert a candy thermometer in the mixture. When it reads 220 degrees F, the jelly is ready.

Remove from the heat. Skim off and discard any surface foam. Ladle the jelly into hot, dry, sterilized jars, filling to within ¼ inch of the rims. Seal with a ⅛-inch-thick layer of melted paraffin (see directions for working with paraffin on page 22). Allow that layer to harden, then add a second layer of the same thickness. Using a damp cloth, wipe the rims clean. Cover with a lid, aluminum foil, or with waxed paper or cotton cloth tightly fastened with twine or a rubber band.

Store in a cool, dark place. The jelly will keep for up to 1 year.

Makes 2 half-pints

Candied Grapefruit Peel

*I*N THIS WINTER CLASSIC, GRAPEFRUIT SLICES IMBIBE SUGAR SYRUP UNTIL THEY ARE SATURATED. IN THE PROCESS THE SLICES TURN FROM PALEST PINK TO AMBER-ROSE, WHILE THE COLOR OF THE SKIN CHANGES FROM YELLOW TO REDDISH ORANGE. ONCE THE PEELS ARE ROLLED IN SUGAR, THEY ARE A TREAT WORTHY OF BEING SERVED AT THE CHRISTMAS PARTY SCENE IN THE NUTCRACKER. IT IS INTRIGUING TO WATCH THE PEELS METAMORPHOSE FROM SOUR, PITHY TRIMMINGS INTO DELECTABLE VICTORIAN CANDIES.

THE AMOUNT OF SUGAR IN THIS RECIPE MAKES A RELATIVELY SOFT PEEL. IF YOU WANT A FIRMER CANDIED PEEL, USE **2** CUPS SUGAR TO MAKE THE SYRUP.

✦

2 large grapefruits,
Ruby or other variety
3 quarts plus 2 cups water
1¹/₂ cups granulated sugar

✦

Cut a thin slice from the top and the bottom of each grapefruit. From the top to the bottom, cut through the outer skin and thick whitish pith to the fruit inside, spacing the cuts abut 1 inch apart. Peel the grapefruits, keeping the skin and pith together.

Cut each of the peel sections lengthwise into long strips ¼ inch wide. You will have about 3 cups. Reserve the fruit for another use.

Pour the 3 quarts water into a saucepan and add the peel strips. Bring the water to a boil over high heat, then reduce the heat to medium. Cook, uncovered, until only an inch or so of water remains in the pan, about 1 hour. Using a slotted utensil, remove the peels from the pan and set them aside in a bowl.

In a stainless-steel or other nonreactive saucepan, combine the 2 cups water with 1 cup of the sugar. Bring to a boil over high heat, stirring until the sugar dissolves.

Remove from the heat and stir the still-warm peels into the syrup. Let the peels stand for 6 or 7 hours at room temperature. Return the pan to low heat and cook the peels until they have absorbed all of the syrup, about 30 minutes. The peels will become translucent and amber. During the last stages of cooking, keep a close eye on the peels to prevent scorching or burning.

Remove the cooked peels from the pan and spread them in a single layer on a piece of aluminum foil or waxed paper. They will be very sticky and supple. Let the peels stand for about 12 hours to dry slightly.

The next day, roll the peels, one by one, in the remaining ½ cup sugar. Leave them at room temperature for 2 to 3 hours to dry. Pack the candied peels into covered tins, boxes, or glass jars in layers separated by waxed paper. Store in a cool, dry place. The peels will keep for up to 2 months.

Makes about 3 dozen pieces

Lemon Curd

LEMON CURD IS AN OPAQUE EGG-
BASED LEMON CUSTARD MOST OFTEN USED AS A
PIE OR TART FILLING. IT IS ALSO GOOD SPREAD ON
WARM SCONES AND OTHER TEA BREADS.

◆

6 egg yolks

1 cup superfine sugar

³/₄ cup fresh lemon juice,
strained (about 5 lemons)

Finely grated zest of 4 lemons

¹/₂ cup unsalted butter,
cut into ¹/₂-inch cubes

◆

Combine the egg yolks
and sugar in the top pan
of a double boiler. Heat
the water in the lower
pan to a simmer; it must
not boil. Using a whisk
beat the yolks and sugar
together until the mix-
ture becomes creamy
and pale and forms thin
strands when dropped
from the edge of a spoon,
about 4 minutes.

Beat in the lemon
juice and zest, then
gradually stir in the
cubes of butter. Continue
to cook, stirring con-
stantly, until the mixture

is quite thick, about 20
minutes. Be careful not
to let the mixture boil, as
the eggs will curdle.

Spoon the hot,
thickened curd into hot,
dry, sterilized jars and
cover with tight-fitting
lids. Store unopened in
the refrigerator for up to
1 month. Once opened
the lemon curd will keep
for up to 1 week.

Makes 2 pints

Confit of Roasted Onions

*T*HIN SHAVINGS OF WHITE WINTER ONIONS COOK DOWN TO A THICK MARMALADE CONSISTENCY WHEN ROASTED IN THE OVEN WITH BUTTER, OLIVE OIL, AND HERBS. THE RESULTING CONFIT MAKES A RUSTIC FARMHOUSE-STYLE SPREAD FOR SANDWICHES OR A GLAZE FOR OTHER VEGETABLES OR MEATS.

◆

4 pounds large white onions

¹/₄ cup butter

¹/₄ cup olive oil

1 teaspoon salt

1 teaspoon granulated sugar

4 fresh or dried bay leaves

*2 tablespoons
chopped fresh thyme leaves*

◆

Preheat an oven to 350 degrees F.

Cut the onions from top to bottom into slices ¼-inch thick. Using the butter, generously grease a baking sheet that is just large enough to hold the sliced onions in a layer 1 inch deep. Add the onions and sprinkle them with the olive oil, salt, sugar, bay leaves, and thyme.

Place the onions in the preheated oven and roast, turning often, until soft and deep golden brown, 45 minutes to 1 hour. Remove from the oven and let cool to room temperature.

Discard the bay leaves. Pack the onions into dry, sterilized jars with lids. Store in the refrigerator. The onions will keep for up to 2 weeks.

Makes about 3 half-pints

Ancho Chili Sauce

Deliciously thick, dark, and slightly smoky, this sauce is particularly good with sharp, somewhat sour fresh cheeses such as goat cheeses. It is equally good with pork, beef, or chicken and with grilled or roasted vegetables. Or use this classic salsa for dipping warm tortillas or crisp corn chips.

◆

3 dried ancho chili peppers

1 tablespoon water,
boiling, or as needed

3 tablespoons
chopped fresh cilantro

¹/₄ cup well-drained
canned plum tomatoes

3 fresh tomatillos, husks removed,
or well-drained canned tomatillos

¹/₄ teaspoon salt

¹/₄ cup safflower
or other vegetable oil

◆

On a griddle or in a dry frying pan over medium heat, place the chilies. Toast lightly on both sides to bring out the flavor of the chilies and to soften the skin. Remove from the griddle or pan and, when cool enough to handle, remove and discard the stems, seeds, and ribs.

Place the chilies in a blender along with 1 tablespoon boiling water and the cilantro. Process to form a thick paste. Add more water if the mixture seems too dry to form a paste. Add the tomatoes, tomatillos, and salt and continue to process until the mixture is very smooth.

In a frying pan over low heat, warm the oil. Add the chile mixture and cook until the mixture thickens, 4 or 5 minutes. Remove from the heat and let cool to room temperature.

Spoon the sauce into a dry, sterilized jar and cover with a tight-fitting lid. Store in the refrigerator for up to 5 days.

Makes ½ pint

*M*ELLOWED BY RED WINE VINEGAR AND AROMATIC HERBS, THE SHARP BITE OF
RAW GARLIC IS DIFFUSED. THE PICKLED CLOVES ARE A FINE ADDITION TO SALAD DRESSING OR
TO ANY DISH THAT CALLS FOR GARLIC.

◆

1 cup peeled garlic cloves

(about 6 large heads)

2 fresh or dried bay leaves

1 teaspoon black peppercorns

1 teaspoon allspice berries

2 or 3 juniper berries

$^1/_2$ to $^3/_4$ cup red wine vinegar

◆

Put the garlic cloves in
a dry, sterilized jar with a
lid. Add the bay leaves,
peppercorns, allspice,
and juniper berries to the
jar and pour in enough
vinegar to cover the
cloves. Cover with the lid.

Store in the refrigera-
tor. The garlic will keep
for up to 4 months.

Makes ½ pint

Pickled Whole Onions

*M*Y BEST MEMORIES OF THESE PICKLED, BITE-SIZE ONIONS ARE AS AN ESSENTIAL COMPONENT OF THE PLOUGHMAN'S LUNCH, THE SIMPLE COLD PLATE SERVED IN PUBS ALL OVER ENGLAND. A WEDGE OF STILTON CHEESE, SLICES OF DARK BREAD, A BIG SPOONFUL OF CHUTNEY, AND A PINT OF THICK, ROBUST BEER COMPLETE THE MEAL.

◆

1 pound boiling onions, about

1½ inches in diameter

3 cups water

1 tablespoon salt

1 teaspoon mace berries

1 teaspoon allspice berries

1 teaspoon whole cloves

2 cinnamon sticks,

each about 4 inches long

6 black peppercorns

3 cups cider vinegar

◆

Remove the skin from each onion, trimming but not cutting off the root cluster at the bottom; the root helps keep the onion intact. In a glass bowl, mix together 2 cups of the water and the salt to make a brine. Add the peeled onions and let stand for 24 hours at room temperature.

The next day, cut out an 8-inch square of cheesecloth. Place in the center the mace and allspice berries, cloves, cinnamon sticks, and peppercorns. Gather up the corners and tie them with kitchen string to make a spice bag.

In a stainless-steel or other nonreactive saucepan bring the vinegar and the remaining cup water to a boil over high heat. Add the spice bag, reduce the heat to medium-low, and simmer for 20 minutes. Discard the spice bag and add the onions. Raise the heat and bring back to a boil, then remove from the heat.

Pack the onions into hot, clean, dry sealable jars with lids. Ladle in the hot vinegar mixture, filling to within ½ inch of the rims. Using a damp cloth, wipe the rims clean. Cover with the lids and process for 40 minutes in a hot-water bath (see instructions for processing hot-pack foods on page 21).

Remove the jars and let them cool for 12 hours or overnight. Check for complete seals.

Store the sealed jars in a cool, dark place. The pickled onions will keep for up to 1 year. Once opened, keep them refrigerated. Store any jar lacking a good seal in the refrigerator for up to 2 weeks.

Makes about 2 pints

*T*HE THIN SHALLOT SLICES TAKE ON A ROSY HUE AFTER SOAKING IN THE RED WINE VINEGAR. THE FINISHED PICKLES CAN BE USED TO MAKE TASTY SPOTS OF COLOR IN SALADS OF ALL KINDS, AND LIKE MANY OTHER TYPES OF PICKLES, GO WELL WITH PLAIN MEATS, BOILED OR ROASTED. CATHERINE BRANDEL, A CHEF AT THE FAMED CHEZ PANISSE IN BERKELEY, CALIFORNIA, SHARED THIS RECIPE WITH ME, WHICH SHE OFTEN PREPARES AT HOME AND AT THE RESTAURANT.

◆

³/₄ pound firm, fresh shallots
³/₄ cup red wine vinegar
¹/₄ cup granulated sugar
¹/₂ cup water
1 fresh or dried bay leaf, bruised
3 or 4 fresh thyme sprigs, bruised

◆

Cut the shallots lengthwise or crosswise into thin slices. Set aside.

In a small stainless-steel or other nonreactive saucepan, combine the vinegar, sugar, water, bay leaf, and thyme. Bring to a boil over high heat. Reduce the heat to medium and simmer for 2 to 3 minutes. Remove from the heat and let cool.

Using a slotted utensil, pack the shallots into dry, sterilized jars with lids. Ladle in the vinegar mixture, filling the jars to within ½ inch of the rims. Cover with the lids.

Store the shallots in the refrigerator for up to 3 weeks.

Makes about 2 half-pints

From left to right:
Pickled Whole Onions
Vin d'Orange
Spicy Lemon Oil
Pickled Garlic Cloves
Pink Pickled Shallots
Pickled Carrots
and Jalapeño Chilies
Confit of Roasted Onions

Pickled Carrots and Jalapeño Chilies

TART, SHARP, AND SPICY, THESE PICKLED CARROTS AND CHILIES PROVIDE JUST THE RIGHT COUNTERPOINT TO RICH-TASTING FOODS. I LIKE TO STACK THESE PICKLES INSIDE A BIG BARBECUED BEEF SANDWICH, DRIPPING WITH SAUCE, OR FOLD A CARROT OR TWO INTO A FRESHLY STEAMED CORN TORTILLA, ON TOP OF CARNE ASADA AND CILANTRO, THEN ADD A LITTLE SALSA.

◆

4 large carrots (about 2 pounds)
1 large white onion
2 fresh jalapeño chili peppers
1¾ cups water
2 teaspoons salt
¾ cup distilled white vinegar
6 black peppercorns

◆

Cut the carrots on the diagonal into slices about ⅜ inch thick. Cut the onion crosswise into slices ¼ inch thick. Slice the chili peppers lengthwise into quarters, remove and discard the stems and seeds.

Put the water and salt in a stainless-steel or other nonreactive saucepan and bring to a boil over high heat. Add the carrots, onion, and chilies and lower the heat to medium. Cook for 4 to 5 minutes. The color of the carrots will become brighter and the onions will become almost transparent. Remove from the heat and mix in the vinegar and peppercorns. Let stand for 12 hours or overnight at room temperature.

The next day, using a slotted utensil, pack the carrots, onions, and chili peppers into dry, sterilized jars with lids. Ladle in the vinegar mixture, filling the jars to within ½ inch of the rims. Cover with the lids. Store in the refrigerator for up to several weeks.

Makes about 2 pints

I WAS QUITE THRILLED WHEN I LEARNED HOW TO MAKE THESE LEMONS, BE-CAUSE THEY HAD ALWAYS SEEMED VERY EXOTIC TO ME. I FIRST SAW THEM—LARGE JARFULS OF THEM—ON THE COUNTER OF A MIDDLE EASTERN DELICATESSEN IN NEW YORK CITY. SEVERAL PEOPLE BOUGHT LEMONS WHILE I WAS THERE. THEY PURCHASED TWO OR THREE AT A TIME, AND THE CLERK DIPPED LONG-HANDLED TONGS INTO THE BIG JARS TO REMOVE THE FRUITS. I HAD NO IDEA HOW THE LEMONS MIGHT BE USED. LATER, I DISCOVERED THEY WERE AN IMPORTANT INGREDIENT IN MIDDLE EASTERN SOUPS AND STEWS, WHERE THEY IMPART A TART, SALTY FLAVOR. I LIKE TO CUT THEM INTO SMALL PIECES AND ADD THEM TO RICH SAL-ADS MADE WITH DUCK, FOR EXAMPLE, OR SERVE THEM AS AN APPETIZER ALONG WITH OLIVES AND SALTED NUTS.

DURING PICKLING, THE LEMONS ABSORB SALT FROM THE BRINE AND ARE FAINTLY FLAVORED BY SPICES. THEY NEED TO SIT FOR ABOUT TWO MONTHS TO BECOME INFUSED WITH THE SEASONINGS BEFORE EATING.

◆

4½ quarts water
7–10 not-overly ripe lemons
⅔ cup sea salt
2 cinnamon sticks,
each about 3 inches long
4 teaspoons coriander seeds
2 teaspoons black peppercorns
8 whole cloves
1 cup olive oil

◆

Pour 3 quarts of the water into a stainless-steel or other nonreactive saucepan. Bring to a boil over high heat and add the lemons. When the water returns to a boil, cook the lemons for 3 to 4 minutes. Drain and immerse the lemons in cold water until they are cool enough to handle. Drain again and set aside.

While the lemons are cooling, prepare the brine. In a saucepan combine the remaining 1½ quarts water and the salt, cinnamon, coriander seeds, peppercorns, and cloves. Bring the mixture to a boil over high heat and then remove from the heat.

Tightly pack the whole lemons into hot, dry, sterilized jars with lids. If you wish, you can halve or quarter the lemons lengthwise to achieve a tighter fit.

Ladle in the hot brine, including the spices, to within ½ inch of the rims. Add the olive oil and cover with the lids.

Store in a cool, dark place. Let stand for 2 months before using, to allow the lemons to take on the flavors of the brine. The lemons will keep for up to 6 months. Once opened, store in the refrigerator.

Makes 2 quarts

*I*N THE LITTLE ADRIATIC TOWN OF CHIOGGIA IN NORTHERN ITALY, I ONCE HAD AN EXTREMELY SIMPLE AND WONDERFUL MEAL. THIS OIL REMINDS ME OF IT.

IT WAS IN FEBRUARY IN THE HEART OF WINTER AND LITTLE FRESH PRODUCE WAS AVAILABLE. THE SMALL FAMILY RESTAURANT WHERE WE ATE HAD NEVERTHELESS MADE A BEAUTIFUL DISPLAY OF THE REGION'S SPECIALTY, RADICCHIO, AND OF LEMONS. NEXT TO THEM SAT LARGE GLASS BOWLS, EACH HOLDING A SHALLOW LAYER OF DARK, GOLDEN GREEN OLIVE OIL SPRINKLED WITH CHOPPED PARSLEY.

WHEN OUR DINNER OF FRIED FISH ARRIVED, IT WAS ACCOMPANIED ONLY WITH A PLATE OF THE BRILLIANT RED-AND-WHITE RADICCHIO LEAVES, ONE OF THE BOWLS OF PARSLEY-TOPPED OLIVE OIL, AND SEVERAL HALVED LEMONS. WE WERE INSTRUCTED BY OUR HOST TO SQUEEZE THE LEMON INTO THE OLIVE OIL, TO ADD A LITTLE SALT AND PEPPER, AND TASTE, ADJUSTING AS NECESSARY. WHEN THE VINAIGRETTE WAS DONE TO OUR SATISFACTION, WE HELPED OURSELVES TO THE RADICCHIO, ADDING IT TO THE BOWL WITH THE VINAIGRETTE AND THEN TOSSING IT WELL.

THIS SPICY OIL CAN BE USED FOR SALAD DRESSINGS, COMPLEMENTS BOILED POTATOES, SAUTÉED CHARD, AND OTHER GREEN VEGETABLES, AND IS GOOD FOR DIPPING BREAD.

❖

2 pounds lemons

2 tablespoons coriander seeds

1 tablespoon black peppercorns

6 fresh lemon leaves

3 fresh or dried bay leaves

4 cups good-quality, fruity olive oil

❖

Cut each lemon into quarters. Put one third of the cut lemons into a dry, sterilized jar with a lid. Sprinkle with about one third of the coriander seeds and peppercorns, 2 lemon leaves, and 1 bay leaf. Repeat the layers twice, then cover with the lid. Let stand for 24 hours in a cool place.

The next day, pour the olive oil into the jar and cover it again. Let stand for 3 days.

At the end of 3 days, remove and discard the lemons. Strain the oil through a sieve lined with several layers of cheesecloth. Decant into a dry, sterilized bottle. Seal with a cork and store the bottle in a cool, dark place. The oil will keep for up to 1 month.

Makes 1 quart

Vin d'Orange

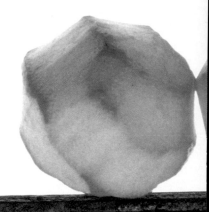

*T*HIS IS A CALIFORNIA VERSION OF
AN OLD FRENCH FARMHOUSE RECIPE FOR A
FLAVORED, FORTIFIED WINE. PEELS FROM EATEN
ORANGES ARE SAVED AND DRIED, THEN TOASTED
IN THE OVEN, FROM WHERE THEY FILL THE HOUSE
WITH AN INTENSE AROMA OF ORANGE OILS.
ALCOHOL, IN THIS CASE VODKA, AND SUGAR ARE
ADDED, ALONG WITH THE ORANGE PEELS, TO A
DRY, ROBUST RED WINE SUCH AS A CALIFORNIA
ZINFANDEL. THE FLAVORED WINE SHOULD REST IN
A COOL, DARK PLACE FOR AT LEAST A MONTH, BUT
THE FLAVORS IMPROVE THE LONGER IT STANDS.

IN MY OPINION, THE PERFECT MOMENT FOR
SERVING A VIN D'ORANGE À LA MAISON APERITIF
WINE IS ON WARM SUMMER NIGHTS, SITTING
OUTSIDE WITH FRIENDS.

✦

Dried peels of 6 small
or 4 large oranges
1 fifth dry red wine,
such as Zinfandel
³/₄ cup granulated sugar
¹/₂ cup vodka

✦

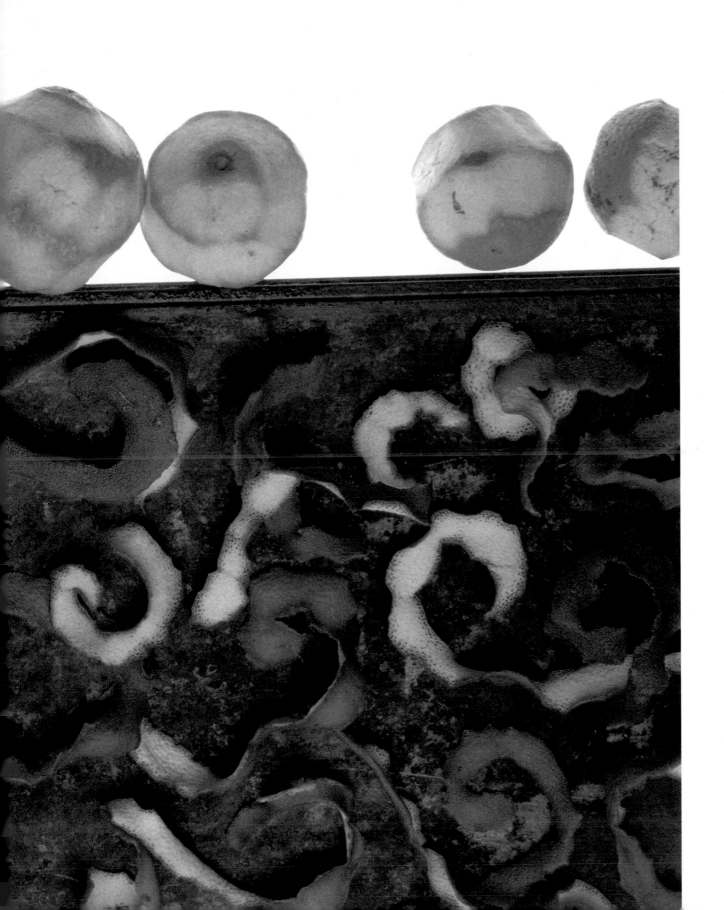

Preheat an oven to 300 degrees F.

Spread the orange peels on a baking sheet. Place in the preheated oven and toast, turning from time to time, until the inner white portion of the peels is golden and the outer skin has deepened to dark orange. This toasting process, which takes about 45 minutes, gives a rich caramel undertone to the wine.

Place the wine, sugar, vodka, and toasted peels in a dry, sterilized widemouthed jar with a lid. Cover with the lid. Store the jar in a cool, dark place, turning it upside down several times a day for a week until the sugar dissolves, then store for at least 1 month but preferably 2 or 3 months.

At this time, strain the wine through a fine-mesh sieve; discard the peels. Decant into dry, sterilized wine or other attractive glass bottles. Cork them and store in a cool, dark place. The wine will keep for up to 1 year.

Makes about 1 quart

Cayenne Walnuts

ENCRUSTED WITH A SPARKLING COAT OF CAYENNE PEPPER, SUGAR, SALT, AND GINGER AND THEN SLOWLY TOASTED IN AN OVEN, THESE SPICY MORSELS REQUIRE LITTLE TIME OR EXPERTISE TO MAKE. THEY ARE SAVORY ADDITIONS TO BOTH GREEN AND FRUIT SALADS— IF THEY AREN'T EATEN OUT OF HAND FIRST.

◆

2 tablespoons cayenne pepper

1¹/₂ teaspoons granulated sugar

1¹/₂ teaspoon salt

³/₄ teaspoon ground ginger

6 egg whites

3 cups walnut halves

(about ³/₄ pound)

◆

Preheat an oven to 225 degrees F.

In a small bowl stir together the cayenne pepper, sugar, salt, and ginger. Place the egg whites in another bowl and, using a whisk or fork, beat until frothy but not stiff. Using a small paint brush or your fingertips, lightly brush each walnut half with a small amount of the egg white and then sprinkle it with some of the cayenne mixture. As each walnut half is coated, place it on a baking sheet.

When all of the walnuts are coated, place the baking sheet in the preheated oven until the nuts are toasted and crunchy and the coating is crisp, 15 to 20 minutes.

Remove from the oven and let the nuts cool completely. Pack the spiced nuts into a covered tin, box, or glass jar. Store in a dry place.

The nuts will keep for up to 3 months.

Makes 3 cups

Salted Blanched Almonds

Raw natural almonds are first briefly soaked in boiling water, and then the thin, papery husks are slipped off, leaving the gleaming, pure ivory nuts unadorned. After being rolled in a little salt, the ivory tones glitter. The fresher the almonds, the more easily the husks will slip off.

◆

4 cups almonds
(about 1 pound)
8 cups water, boiling
4 egg whites
1 cup fine salt

◆

Put the almonds in a bowl and pour the boiling water over them. Let stand for 1 minute, then drain. Using your fingers, gently rub the brown skins until they slip off the nuts. If the skins don't slip off easily, once again pour boiling water over the nuts. This time, let the nuts stand only 30 seconds, just long enough to loosen the skins, then drain and skin.

Place the egg whites in a small bowl and, using a whisk or fork, beat until frothy but not stiff. Using a small paint brush or your fingertips, lightly brush a little of the egg white on each almond and then sprinkle with salt. If you use too much egg white, the salt will adhere thickly, making for a very salty— perhaps too salty—nut. As the nuts are salted, place them in a single layer on waxed paper and let dry for several hours or overnight.

Store in covered tins, boxes, or glass jars in a cool, dry place. The nuts will keep for 2 to 3 months.

Makes 4 cups

ACKNOWLEDGMENTS

There are numerous people behind the words, the thoughts, and the photographs that make this book more than the sum of its parts. Our heartfelt thanks to them all:

To Michaele Thunen for her generous help throughout the seasons of this volume. To Jacqueline Jones for her light touch with our work and her beautiful designs. To Kristen Jester for always being at hand when needed. To Michele Miller for her unending support and assistance. To Dimitri Spathis for his assistance. To editor Bill LeBlond at Chronicle Books for his clear vision, creativity, and understanding. To Sharon Silva for her careful and thoughtful editing of the manuscript. To Ed Haverty for his help throughout. To my daughter, Ethel Brennan, for the enthusiasm and professionalism she brought to the task of recipe testing. To my husband, Jim Schrupp, who reads every word I write and eats everything I cook. To Oliver Brennan and Tom and Dan Schrupp who are my most discerning culinary critics. And to Karen Frerichs for her cheerful and professional assistance in recipe testing. A special thanks to my agent, Susan Lescher.

Especially from Kathryn: Deep thanks to my husband, Michael Schwab, and my boys, Eric and Peter, for their love and support.

For produce, linens, ribbons, and other sundries:

A special thanks to Bill Fujimoto at Monterey Market in Berkeley. To Stuart Dixon of Stonefree Farms in Davis and Watsonville, for giving us the freedom to roam his fields to collect tomatoes, sweet peppers, herbs, and greens. To Frank Martin and his sister, Madeline Jimenez, fruit growers in Winters, for the cherry-laden branches they gave us, and to Knoll Organic Farms in Brentwood for the purple artichokes they shipped to us when Georgeanne's garden crop had finished. To Anna Le Blanc for giving us rose and lemon clippings from her Berkeley yard whenever we asked, and to Leonard and Nancy Becker who gifted us with oranges on branches. To Susan Kirshenbaum for her beautiful calligraphy on jar labels.

To Betty Jane Roth, of Chico, who loaned us antique linens and kitchen utensils, as did Carla Nasaw of Ross, and in Berkeley, to Mimi Luebbermann who let us use her antique silver flatware and jars and Devorah Nussenbaum who allowed us to delve into her ribbon collection.

Many of the props that appear in these pages are available at the following stores:

Ribbons and ornaments:
Tail of the Yak,
Berkeley, California;
Bell'occhio,
San Francisco, California

Antique linens:
Lacis,
Berkeley, California

Garden and tabletop accessories:
The Gardener,
Berkeley, California

Canning jars and accessories:
Sur la Table,
Seattle, Washington

Antique canning jars:
Clementine's,
Chico, California

Antique kitchenware:
Bonnie Grossman,
Ames Gallery,
Berkeley, California

BIBLIOGRAPHY

Brennan, Georgeanne, Isaac Cronin and Charlotte Glenn. *The New American Vegetable Cookbook.* Reading, Massachusetts: Aris Books/Addison-Wesley, 1985.

Carey, Norma. *Perfect Preserves.* New York: Stewart, Tabori & Chang, Inc., 1990.

McGee, Harold. *On Food and Cooking.* New York: Scribner's Sons, 1984.

Medecin, Jacques. *Cuisine du Comté de Nice.* Paris: Julliard, 1972.

Reboul, J.B. *La Cuisinière Provençale.* 6th ed., Marseille: Tacussel, 1985.

Sorzio, Angelo. *Le Conserve.* Milan: Gruppo Editoriale Fabbri, 1983.

Time-Life. *Preserving.* Alexandria, Virginia: Time-Life Books, 1981.

INDEX

TABLE OF EQUIVALENTS

The exact equivalents in the following tables have been rounded for convenience.

Equivalents for Common Ingredients

US / UK

oz = ounce
lb = pound
in = inch
ft = foot
tbl = tablespoon
fl oz = fluid ounce
qt = quart

METRIC

g = gram
kg = kilogram
mm = millimeter
cm = centimeter
ml = milliliter
l = liter

WEIGHTS

US / UK	Metric
1 oz	30 g
2 oz	60 g
3 oz	90 g
4 oz (¼ lb)	125 g
5 oz (⅓ lb)	155 g
6 oz	185 g
7 oz	220 g
8 oz (½ lb)	250 g
10 oz	315 g
12 oz (¾ lb)	375 g
14 oz	440 g
16 oz (1 lb)	500 g
1½ lb	750 g
2 lb	1 kg
3 lb	1.5 kg

OVEN TEMPERATURES

Fahrenheit	Celsius	Gas
250	120	½
275	140	1
300	150	2
325	160	3
350	180	4
375	190	5
400	200	6
425	220	7
450	230	8
475	240	9
500	260	10

LIQUIDS

US	Metric	UK
2 tbl	30 ml	1 fl oz
¼ cup	60 ml	2 fl oz
⅓ cup	80 ml	3 fl oz
½ cup	125 ml	4 fl oz
⅔ cup	160 ml	5 fl oz
¾ cup	180 ml	6 fl oz
1 cup	250 ml	8 fl oz
1½ cups	375 ml	12 fl oz
2 cups	500 ml	16 fl oz
4 cups / 1 qt	1 l	32 fl oz

BROWN SUGAR

¼ cup	1½ oz	45 g
½ cup	3 oz	90 g
¾ cup	4 oz	125 g
1 cup	5½ oz	170 g
1½ cups	8 oz	250 g
2 cups	10 oz	315 g

WHITE SUGAR

¼ cup	2 oz	60 g
⅓ cup	3 oz	90 g
½ cup	4 oz	125 g
¾ cup	6 oz	185 g
1 cup	8 oz	250 g
1½ cups	12 oz	375 g
2 cups	1 lb	500 g

RAISINS / CURRANTS / SEMOLINA

¼ cup	1 oz	30 g
⅓ cup	2 oz	60 g
½ cup	3 oz	90 g
¾ cup	4 oz	25 g
1 cup	5 oz	155 g

JAM / HONEY

2 tbl	2 oz	60 g
¼ cup	3 oz	90 g
½ cup	5 oz	155 g
¾ cup	8 oz	250 g
1 cup	11 oz	345 g